RETRACED:

Love Can't Wait

A story told by Marcus and Sheyla…

By Anthony Cuffie

Copyright © 2004 by Anthony Cuffie

Retraced
by Anthony Cuffie

Printed in the United States of America

ISBN 1-594676-89-5

All rights reserved solely by the author. The author guarantees all contents are original and do not infringe upon the legal rights of any other person or work. No part of this book may be reproduced in any form without the permission of the author. The views expressed in this book are not necessarily those of the publisher.

www.xulonpress.com

DEDICATIONS

I've lost many friends to the streets living on the eastside of Detroit. My mother, Linda Cuffie knowing what was out there, protected me from myself. When I wanted to be a part of the "in crowd," she directed me towards Christ; I resisted, but in the end, after careful study, and soul searching, and Him revealing himself to me; I've come to know him for myself. My mother treasured every relationship she had, and loved people unconditionally, even when people used her. The only thing that hurts me about her death is that it now will take my death to see her again. Mom, your Ant-Ant loves you like no other son in this world and I thank you for being my mother.

> Love always,
> Ant-Ant

To all my boys from the eastside of Detroit, from Palmer to Kirby street, to the Brewster Projects dead or locked up. I hope that your memories have shown what wrong and right decisions can do to life with so much promise. The essence of your being will always be missed. Experiences, circumstances, and people are like ingredients mixed together to help those connected develop into who they become. I'll always cherish the memories of our dreams, hopes, and passions. For others, I shall continue to carry the torch and break stereotypes. Cats like me can come from the hood, make it out, support and give back to the community their from! Stay up fellas.

To my Grams and Granddad (Robert Sr. and Elizabeth Cuffie),

All I remember is unconditional love and strength. You carried the family on your backs and never asked for anything in return. What you meant and mean to me is indescribable; I miss you both so much! Even in death, you live.

I can't forget my beloved late Uncle Mason, and my beloved late Aunt Ida.

love always!

-This is a work of fiction. Names, characters, places and incidents either are the product of the author's imagination or are used fictitiously, and any resemblance to any actual persons, living or dead, events or locales is entirely coincidental.

ACKNOWLEDGEMENTS

The closeness of the Cuffie family has kept me strong in the midst of turmoil and storms. God has blessed us, and I thank all of you in Michigan and Georgia, etc.! Pastor Robert Cuffie Jr., Aunt Angie, keep being sweet. Truly, you both represent the Most High God! Cynthia Cuffie-Baker and Leonard, your support doesn't go without great appreciation. Aunt Eva, your long life and inspiration carries many to the understanding of God's grace upon those who follow truth. Aunt Frances, I love you. To my sisters Lakia and Deshonda Cuffie we are the branches and extension of momma. Christ must always remain #1 in our lives. I can't thank you guys enough for helping me out when I needed you most. To my uncle or should I say my brother, Darrin Christopher Cuffie and Aunt Dee, Thanks. Uncle David and Aunt Sally, mad love to you! My Pops, you be blessed, love you! To my step dad, all has been forgiven, mad love to you. Pastor Lenell Caldwell, thanks for introducing me to the drums at a young age.

To the Williams family, Betty, Joyce, Peggy, I love you all. Thank you for accepting me for me with all my imperfections. To all my cousins, I will always treasure you: Amber,

Zakiya, Camesha, Gabriel, Daniel, Christa, Jordan, Matthew, Kamaal, Robert, Latoya, Ariel, Delmarco (Cuz4life), Diane, Lashonda, Shalonda, Kelly, Al, Charlie, La'sha, Queenesta, Grandma Orangie, Ann Janette, Dezarah, Sherry, Eric and Derrick, The Riley Fam, Tamika, Mi Mi(Ronda), Little Butch(Ronald), Lisa, Karen, Beverly, Deborah and Kim, all my aunts and uncles and many more.

To my dawgs, my homies, my friends:
    Starting with two of the tri-factor Dannie Hayes, Flinnoia Hall. Derrick Hayes(lil'bro), and their wives, you have shown me what friendship is all about; I feel like y'all be my brothas. Excuse my vernacular, but there aren't better words to describe our closeness. Steve Reeves, man you are a friend that I look up to (Roz, Mrs. Reeves, you're a great Godmother); friendship means so much to you and it's demonstrated through your love; you have no idea of how you've positively affected my life. Jason Bell/Devonna thank you for being there. Thanks to Robert and Min Yon Brooks, Wilmonie (one of the most talented vocalist in the world), my music partner and his wife Janita Page, Katu Davis, Nut(Ahmed Green), Nookie, Devon, Sunse, Jeff Ragland, Money Wayne, The Collier Fam, Nique, Boo, Marcus Robinson, Monifah, Pastor Mike and Joslyn Carter, (my other mom) Kim Norris, the 1990 Murray Wright Family, Kennedy Family, the Ferris State University Family, and the Christian Business Network. Oh yeah, Renda Horne, thank you for your encouragement and your gift of writing for the body of Christ. If I've forgotten any names, please charge it to my head and not my heart.

To the Hood family:
    My brother-and sister-in-laws are true to the word family. These are my family members: Tony, Lawrence, Nyree, Mary. You guys are blessings and gifts in my life.

Retraced

My mother-and father-in-law took me in as one of their own; I love you guys so much for making me feel like your blood. I love you for everything you are to me. Granddad and Grandma Hood, I love you so much, including: John, Dale, Billy, Tommy and Ann, Todd, Ronald, the late Clinton Hood Jr., and many more. Oh yeah, I can't forget the Swanson Family and Erlene and James Hawkins. Nieces and Nephews: Jade, T.J., Lauryn, Lanya, lil Marvin

To my Church Family:
Pastor James and Sister Morman are blessings to our lives. Thank you for being true examples of what God is calling us all to be. The peace and love that's at our church filters down from the head. To the rest of the Christian 'The Tab' Tabernacle Church, I love you all deeply. Fred and Courtney Berry, a special shout out goes to you guys for being true friends.

To my Mrs. Precious, the best hair stylist in Da'twa:
My wife, Paula Hood-Cuffie is more than a gift. She's my twin, my strength, my lover, my friend, my backbone, my soulmate, and much more. Thank you for involving yourself in the vision. I pray that God continues to lead us to our purpose with many, many, many, many, many, many years together before leaving this earth. To my sons Michael and Kylin, daddy loves you very much. Both of you are joys in my life. Coming home just to have you boys jump on me and smiling is a gift that nourishes the soul.

Special thanks goes to Janice Sykes, Ann Gist, and Vanessa Harley, Demitra Wilson – the panelist that reviewed the pre-advanced copy. And to all the guest artist on the Soundtrack.

The Beginning

As the siren blared, she regained consciousness and realized a man was taking her pulse, asking her questions that she couldn't quite make out. Kim felt blood dripping from her forehead and a burning, throbbing pain between her legs. Everything happening so fast, when she came to the realization she was in an ambulance. The only thought that entered her mind was, "what happened?"

Earlier, after a long day of waitressing, Shannon asked Kim to go to the club with her. Kim agreed on the premise that they did not make it an all nighter. The party was at its peak. Everyone was dressed nicely at Blaze, Detroit's finest club. In this city, you didn't leave the house for anything without showcasing your finest gear. Kim's outfit was no different; her guise screamed for attention and so did she.

Kim possessed a beauty that made any married man or woman feel vulnerable and insecure. Her light green eyes glowed with every stare. Her bronze, blemish free skin, complimented her full flawless lips. Her hair caressed her shoulders, bouncing with every movement. And her body, lean with curves, defined true perfection. Men craved Kim and she knew it. This was her night to relieve some of

Retraced

life's strain. Obviously her friend Shannon had plans to relieve some stress of her own by partying like a wild women. She was all over the floor, hugging and grinding on every man that winked. This spelled trouble, because Kim knew that men started looking at her as if she was down for whatever, too.

The crowd got bigger, and became more rowdy. A young man pulled Kim onto the dance floor. Reluctantly she danced with him because she feared what he would do. His breath reeked with alcohol, mixed with a peppermint to cover the smell. He was perfumed with the fragrance of marijuana and the hearty man danced with her as if he owned her. As he constantly rubbed his pelvis against her flesh, she yelled for him to stop. He ignored her and drew her closer to his sweaty body telling her he wanted to make her his wife. She slapped him and he immediately hawked up mucous and spit on her. As she wiped her face and ran away from him, she felt another pair of hands caressing her thighs. She couldn't tell from what direction it came, but she knew it was time to go. Immediately embarrassment and feelings of violation overwhelmed her; she had never felt so humiliated in her life.

Kim found Shannon and explained the situation and begged Shannon to drive her home. Shannon, enjoying herself, responded out of agitation, "What's up with you, this is the livest party of the year, you're blowing my high." Kim ran outside consuming the fresh air. She was embarrassed and ticked off at her friend Shannon, the one person she thought she could trust. As she slowly walked down the street to the bus station, the night was cool, and very quiet.

The earth stood still as if nothing on the planet interrelated. This night was ending terribly and who could imagine it would get worse. The click-clack, click-clack of her heels leaped off the cement as her feet hit the pavement. The more her heart beat, the faster the sound trampled the ground. She felt very uneasy as she stood waiting on the bus. As Kim pulled out a cigarette, she suddenly felt a hand cover her mouth and her fears materialized. Every bit of strength she could muster up wasn't enough to fight off the man. His vigor was too much for her to overcome.

As the man punched her, he screamed, "I got a gun. I'll use it if you keep puttin' up a fight." To weaken her, he kneed her in the stomach. The ski-masked tyrant was very muscular and began to pull her inside a nearby abandoned building. After ripping each article of clothing off her body, the man forcefully visited her inner being. She cried inside, finding it hard to breathe, her muscles tightened and she stared into unconsciousness. He continued to thrust himself on Kim, as if she was enjoying him, he whispered in her ear, "I love you baby, you love me?" When he finished, he said he was sorry and reacted as if he'd grasped what he did was wrong.

Fighting out of the daze of unconsciousness, she saw her violator zip up his pants and run away. Kim struggled to her knees, dazed about everything that happened and staggered towards the nightclub. As the club was letting out, Shannon walked out and immediately noticed her friend Kim bewildered and bloody in torn clothes whimpering disturbingly. Shannon rushed to her side. While caressing her, she let out a remorseful cry and Kim collapsed in her arms.

Nine and a half months later, Kim had a baby girl, whom she kept out of confusion and loneliness. Her name was Sheyla.

SHEYLA......

Ring. Ring. Hello! "Hey mom, can you watch Sheyla for me?" My mom asked my grandmother this question all the time. "Oh girl," she replied, "ain't you 'bout tired of asking me to raise your daughter. Seven years have passed and you're still acting like a teenager. Now momma's tired, where are you going?"

"Come on mom, me and T.C. need some time together. We're trying to keep things together."

"Why y'all need time together when he lives there," she asked sarcastically.

"Look! It's not your business, I'm just asking for a favor. Can you help me out momma?"

"Kim, momma loves you, but I'm your hindrance," She paused, " I'm there for all of your failures and if I continue being your parachute, you'll never understand that the fall can hurt you."

That Hated Boyfriend

My mother immediately slammed the phone in grandma's ear and told T.C. they didn't have a babysitter. T.C. is the boyfriend that my mom loved and I hated. His eyes were intense and were set close on his face. His face had a permanent frown, giving the impression that he was always about business. He spoke with an accent and slurred his words, which made it difficult to understand him. He walked around the house with a slow methodical strut, sneaking up on people like an animal preying on the attack. T.C.'s full name is Terry Clemons and he's known for all the dirt he's done in the 'hood. It's even rumored that he once robbed a bank all by himself. Many said he was responsible for most of the drive-by's in the area. Everyone feared T.C.

Right after the rape, moms refused to date and was a scared nervous wreck. T.C. put the mack down and tricked my mom into a relationship, telling her he wouldn't let anyone ever harm her again, his presence demanded respect and she liked that. He had a way of handling situations. My mom was worshipped in the hood because of her new man's reputation.

After finding out that they couldn't drop me off at

grandma's, he was hysterical and punched a hole in the wall, screaming obscenities. I was accustomed to witnessing this kind of behavior. The smallest things ticked him off. I was scared of T.C. and hated that mom did any and everything to please and keep him around. T.C. said, "I'm out, let's go, just leave her here." Like a slave to abuse, mom ran after him leaving me in the house by myself. Me, a little girl. Frantic with hysteria, I yelled, "Mom, please don't leave me, please, I'm scared!" The torture of constant abuse had my stomach trembling, my head bursting with pressure, hurt from the feeling of being abandoned. I called Grandma or should I say Grams, as I affectionately called her, to tell her what happened.

"What! How could she do that? I'll be over in a second." My grandmother had dropped me and moms off on a number of occasions, but she had never been invited inside the house. Thirty minutes after the phone call, Grams was at the door. I opened the door crying, as if I'd witnessed a murder. I fell against her shoulders embracing her, Grams told me not to worry about anything.

Our house was a cramped two-bedroom bungalow, infested with roaches and a stench that smelled like someone decided to fertilize the carpet. It was truly a disgusting sight. I was always embarrassed to invite friends over, because our house had to be the worst one in the neighborhood. The rooms were dark, hiding our beat down sofa that had seat pillows hiding the fact that there were no springs underneath. My grams sat on the sofa and fell right through to the floor. She hopped up, and her bottom lipped sagged as her eyes wandered around surveying the whole scenery. She nodded her head and yelled for me to hurry up.

We went to my room to gather some clothes and rushed out of the house. On the ride back to Grams' house, devastated by what she had witnessed, she cried. I was her only grandchild. Grams proceeded to speak in a strange language, that I now know as another tongue, ending it with, "Lord Jesus get us through this." Whenever she did that Jesus stuff I was embarrassed, but this time I understood that this was her way of getting through her problems. She repeated over and over again, "Where did I go wrong? Where did I go wrong?" She had put so much work in as a single parent, gave mom all the love she could, yet mom decided to make her God Mr. Terry Clemons.

That day driving home to Grams' house was a blur because she was troubled and I was upset. How could her daughter be so irresponsible, she thought out aloud. Grams loved her some Kim, but their relationship had been strained since T.C. came into the picture. Grams understood the emotional tragedies mom faced in the past, but dealing with T.C. was a deep thing for her. Anger compelled the old lady to hold her tongue back, not to say anything out of the way in front of me. She burst into tears of frustration. "Grams, what's wrong?" I asked out of concern. "Nothing baby, nothing at all."

After leaving me, T.C. and mom picked up my cousin Teeka. She often hung out with them. Teeka left them early to come tell my Grams what had happened. Mom told T.C. that she felt bad about leaving me. "Anything could have happened, she's only seven." T.C. responded calmly with his face twisted up, "Gurl, chill out, it ain't that bad, it's her bed time anyway. She know to go to sleep. You having labor pains without being pregnant." "What," mom frantically asked. "You making sum' en out of nuthin, now chill," he responded. "But," Mom started to speak. Smack!!! Mom's face now bore T.C.'s handprint.

She started to cry. T.C. looked at her and said, "Baby, I'm sorry, but you talk too much. This night is ar' night, not Sheyla's, not yo momma's, but ar' night." T.C. was like an assassin's bomb, unexpectedly going off. Overhearing Teeka telling my grandmother this story deepened my hate for T.C.

He somehow found contentment in his own madness. Apparently, they ended up at the movie theater, where he held and cuddled with mom, as if everything was okay.

Grams didn't react to this news. It was like she had come to the realization that she couldn't continue to stress herself out about her grown daughter. Desperate to make sure I wouldn't fall into the same traps as my mom, Grams was eager to do whatever she could to get me out of my dysfunctional home.

Even though things weren't great, I wasn't ready to leave mom because I was worried that she would be killed if I left. For some strange reason I felt like my presence protected my mom, even T.C. wouldn't kill her in front of me. He was crazy, but there were some things I believed he just wouldn't do.

Growing up, I could only remember promising myself that I wouldn't end up like my mother. I dreamed the All-American dream; three kids, a white house with a picket fence and a loving husband. The reality of this truly happening was slim. I mean, coming from the hood, who makes it out? Everything was against me, and growing up with T.C. as the head of our household was slighting my chances the more. He was the only male example I had in my life!

Bonny and Clyde Love

June 13 was a big day for me, I had just graduated from elementary school and was on my way to junior high. Mom planned this big celebration, supposedly for me, but it was also T.C.'s 37th birthday, so she invited mostly T.C.'s peeps. T.C's oldest brother, John, declined the invitation. John had recently been released from prison after serving six years for a crime that T.C. committed. T.C shot an old lady, trying to steal her purse. She didn't die and was able to give the cops a description of the suspect. They picked John up a week later, having two other witnesses placing him at the scene of the crime. He and T.C. look just alike. They both have the same build, color and similar mannerisms. John had been in trouble before, but nothing like this. T.C. never came forward to get his brother off, he never wrote, apologized or called. John's pain grew into a deep hate for his brother. This situation caused the entire Clemons family to resent T.C., which explains why his other siblings never showed or responded to the invitation. His mom and dad are deceased, but I heard they too weren't happy with their oldest son before they died.

Six of T.C's closest friends came to the party, Calvin the

Pimp, Tre, Bars, R.J., Bobby and Lil D. Calvin was T.C's best friend; he was down for whatever. Calvin wasn't really a pimp, he got the name because he titled his clothes and cars as being 'pimped out'. He was always seen with a different girl, and the only kind of girls he attracted were girls who were of course, 'pimped out'. Lisa was his new honey. This was the second time I had seen her and Calvin had talked about her like she was "the one."

"Hey Calvin, is this going to be my new aunt," I asked just to be nosy. "Sheyla, it might be, it just might be," Calvin whispered in my ear.

She had on an outfit that didn't fit and showed nothing but her voluptuousness. She flung her parts everywhere, looking very easy, just like a prostitute begging for someone to pick her up. Cal, short for Calvin, spit every time he talked. He always had a new way to make millions, he was a trip! Surprisingly, three of mom's friends came through. She had to beg them until they finally decided to come, but on the understanding that they were there to support mom's little girl. They hated T.C. and knew he was bad news. T.C. hated them too, but was happy that they came over for the celebration.

T.C. was crazy, finicky, and just hard to figure out. During the party, Cal was telling his money scheme to everyone, spitting as usual. " Man we can get on, all we need is a few grand to start off." "Start off to do what," asked Lil. D? "Well, high school basketball is becoming a big thing to bet on. I figure we can get some money together to buy off some of the star players." "For what," replied Lil D.

Calvin responded with "dummy, we can get them to throw the games and we can bet big dollars against them." "Man, that'll never work," T.C. said. Cal had this serious look and was disappointed that no one was feeling him.

Wine bottles clattered together signifying another one. These dudes were putting alcoholic drinks down, left and right. As the night continued, it didn't stop anyone from adding to his or her drunkenness. They began telling old stories about their past. T.C. never opened his mouth, like he was scared he might confirm many of the rumors. He didn't trust anyone. Cal kind of hinted towards the topic of the solo bank robbery, referring to the rumor about T.C. robbing the local Comerica Bank. T.C. immediately told Cal to shut up.

Cal was a straight-up jokester. He found humor in everything. Cal went around telling everyone that they smelled like they wanted to be alone. He was cracking himself up and me too. Hey, I thought he was funny. T.C. was walking around with his butt-crack showing. Every time he walked past Cal, Cal let out a fart sound, laughing. Man he was killing me! T.C. had no idea of what everyone was laughing about. "What's up with ya'll! Fools drinking too much," T.C. said. The more he felt left out of the joke, the angrier he became, which usually spelled trouble. T.C. caught a slight draft run across his lower back, so he pulled up his pants. Everyone saw this, then glanced at Cal. Cal was holding his nose as to say it was too late, T.C. had stunk up the room. Immediately a burst of laughs screamed out. People were on the floor laughing. I mean boo-hooing. A loud "shut up" wrung out! T.C. stood over Cal, "I mean it nigga, don't play me!" T.C. had a look on his face that could kill.

Everyone saw that this wasn't a laughing matter and the room went to a whisper because it was no secret on what his anger could lead to. I was trippin, because it was apparent T.C. had something much stronger than alcohol in his system. Lisa, Cal's girl was holding her laugh because she thought the whole thing was hilarious. She couldn't hold it in any longer. "Ha ha ha ha, hee, hee, heeeeeeeee woooo exploded from her lips.

Why did she do that? T.C. immediately turned and ran up on Lisa. He swung his hand behind his head and let it go. A straight back-hand smack on Lisa's jaw. She screamed

Retraced

and ran out of the house crying. Everything from that point went into a frantic state, it was as if I was having an out-of-body experience. Cal making an attempt to defend his girlfriend, pushed T.C. and yelled, "Man what's up?" T.C. looked, smirked, then pulled out his silver 357 Mag. Everyone's eyes widened. He aimed the gun at Cal's head and shot once. A sharp "No, what are you doing?" lurked in the air as all the women roared in fear! He followed up the first shot by standing over him saying, "Dawg, I told you not to go dare wit' me."

Another shot, then another rung out. T.C. blasted large holes in his best friend's chest. Our couch, soaked in blood, had a permanent imprint where Cal's body ricocheted onto the floor. For a second, complete silence deadened the place. I couldn't keep my eyes off of Cal. The way he pounced on the floor, the sound of his head hitting the wood foundation will never leave my mind. I slowly turned to T.C., and started screaming at the top of my lungs. Mom grabbed me, "Come on baby, get your things."

After retrieving everything I could grab in a plastic bag, we slipped on a puddle of blood as we ran to the front room. T.C. was still in shock about what he had done, sobbing, "Man why did you make me lose it, now look at you, look at you!! After regrouping, he told Mom to roll out with him. T.C. started mumbling, "We gotta get outta town." He hit the steering wheel. "Baby, can you believe Cal tripped on me like that?" "No baby," momma said with a trembling light voice. I knew she was scared, but I thought this was our chance to escape T.C. and his craziness. Boy, I was wrong. "We're going to drop off Sheyla over yo mutha's house, and bust up outta state," T.C. said as he tried to regroup. Realizing what he was saying; I erupted, "No mom, you can't leave, please don't, mommy, no!" Outside of Grams, momma was all I had. Mom was crying. It was palpable she was sick with the idea of leaving her baby. She handed me a letter to give to Grams explaining why she was leaving me. Moms' passion and love for T.C. overpowered her and she chose him over me. As the car drove off, tears fell, while I stared in a trance wondering what was next. I stood there for a long time before I rang the doorbell, feeling left to die and unloved.

Life with Grams

My grandmother was an older looking version of my mother. For a woman that was considered old, she sure was gorgeous. I always wondered why she never dated. She hadn't been on a date since my grandfather died some years ago. As she always said, her boyfriend was Jesus and according to her, that's all she needed.

Le Ann Patron, my grandmother, was very independent and caring. I never knew momma's past, but I always wondered why she did some of the things she did. I never had the heart to ask my Grams. Looking at some of my mother's old pictures, promiscuous behavior was written all over her. "Baby, I promise I won't make some of the same mistakes I made raising your mother. You won't be a little hoochie momma," Grams gently spoke as she kissed my forehead.

The first day of school came around. It had been approximately three months since the last time I'd seen or heard from my mother. I was truly worried, because all kinds of crazy thoughts came to my head. Where was she? Did T.C. kill her, too? Is she in jail with T.C.? I mean everyday was filled with disbelief about what happened. T.C.'s perplexed mind could lead him to the most violent acts.

The transition of my living arrangements changed so much. Living with Grams came with too many rules. We went to church at least two to three times a week. It was strange, because most of the members were some of the craziest people I had ever met. Take sister Gina for instance, whenever the Pastor said God is good, she'd jump, scream and start speaking in tongues, like she was speaking Spanish. It reminded me of when Grams did it. I used to get in trouble because whenever I saw her do this, I rolled, laughing as if someone was tickling me.

Staring and watching people in church was as entertaining as going to see Eddie Murphy do stand up. Man, I didn't get one thing out of church. Our Pastor was wacked out. He was always huffing and puffing, breathing all hard. Every word was directly read out of the Bible. I didn't even understand the Bible, so what was his purpose? My mind often wandered off to what I was going to do after this circus was over. Another thing that got me was that it was known that the pastor was sleeping with half the women in the church.

Had it not been for Grams, I wouldn't even believe in God because she was one person I could say who really did live what she believed. Nothing could derail her from she and her Jesus. I often felt sorry for her because I thought Jesus was her crutch, especially since she was lonely and getting older. I wondered what made her continue attending that hypocritical church. Greater Praise of Truth and Life. One day I asked her, "Grams why do you stay at Greater Praise of Truth and Life?" She immediately responded with, "Shey, I don't serve man. God is God, no matter what a man is or does, so that's who I serve." That was the craziest nonsense I had ever heard, but loyalty, love and forgiveness was something that Grams was all about. I really didn't understand or appreciate her faith until I got older.

Grams had this best friend that she spent a lot of time

with, Mrs. Caroline. She was a full figured lady with a beautiful face. Mrs. Caroline was always singing around the house. Her voice was a sound of glory. If she couldn't do anything else, she could sure sing and cook. Mrs. Caroline had recently obtained custody of her deceased daughter's son. Grams decided this particular Sunday she would try to make the boy's transition with his grandmother easy by introducing him to a friend, me. "Sheyla, this is Marcus, Marcus this is Sheyla," Mrs. Caroline said with a grin.

"What's up Marcus?"

"How are you Sheyla?" he replied. "I'm Marcus Stunson; my boys call me Stun." In my mind, I was thinking more like runt. He was puny. Poor thing, he had this fake gold chain on that looked half yellow, half green. Who or what was he trying to impress?

"Okay, ya'll go in the basement and play the Nintendo game system, while grown folk talk," Mrs. Caroline said. While in the basement, blank space peered between Marcus and I, so I decided to initiate some kind of conversation.

"So what do you do for fun?" I asked.

"Well, all I do is hoop. My basketball is my best friend. It's always by my side and I can make it do whatever I want it to do," he answered. It was obvious to me that this kid wasn't playing with a full deck or he was a straight up busta. Basketball was cool, even though I was in junior high school, but most bruh's in my hood considered feeling girls behinds, selling drugs and video games as their pastimes.

"So Stun, are you any good at playing Mario Brothers," I asked.

"Naw, not really."

"You really don't talk much do you," I said.

"A little, but," he paused.

"But what? I asked. "Nothing." I didn't want to dig in, so I let it go. I noticed him staring in my eyes. I wasn't conceited, but a lot of guys liked me. My mom's friends

Retraced

would always say how beautiful I was and that I looked just like my mother did when she was my age, so I knew he was digging me. But there was no way that I was going to give him any reason to act on his feelings.

For one, he was a puny runt and for some strange reason I was always hooked on boys that stayed in trouble. Plus Grams wasn't keen on boys hanging around me, that's why I couldn't understand why she wanted me to befriend this Stun kid. "What happened to your, I'm the man attitude you had upstairs," I asked. He said, "Well, that's not really me. It's just when I saw your pictures and then saw you, I thought it was a good way to introduce myself to someone that was so pretty."

For someone to be so young, even back then, Marcus had a way with words. That night ended with me feeling like I had a nice little friend, like a brotha I never had.

At home Grams asked me if Marcus was a nice kid. I said "Yeah, pretty cool, just quiet." She went on to tell me that Marcus had some issues with his mom, and that his mom wasn't the best parent, and she was no longer around. I wanted her to elaborate, but me being a kid, she was only going to say so much. Whatever the situation, it couldn't have been worse than my family drama. I mean my mother was running and hiding out with a murderer that attracted trouble wherever he went. Just knowing my grams, I concluded that my grandmother felt Marcus and I could help each other get through our similar dilemmas. I wanted to ask Grams how to deal with me missing my mother so much, but I knew she was going to say Jesus this, God that. I mean, her words often kept me stranded, looking for more answers, so I was better off to just pray my own prayers and seek answers in other ways.

Dear God,
Why is all this drama left for me to deal with? I'm too

young. Please take care of my mother. Do something bad to T.C., so moms can come back home. I really, really miss her. Oh yeah, can you send Grams a husband, I know she's lonely, even if she won't admit it.

Amen.

This was one of my many prayers. I prayed with no expectancy that anything would happen. To me, God, Santa Claus, and The Tooth Fairy were all the same. I mean, who really got what they asked for? The next day began with me being late for school. It was a day that I wouldn't forget because it sparked my beginning of straight-up-foolishness. At school, during third hour, we had gym and I was late putting on my gym clothes, which consisted of shorts and a t-shirt that revealed my developing body. My curves wasn't nothing compared to my best friends.

My girl Latasha, better known as Tash, was something else. She's been my friend since we were little chillins. Her moms and mine hung out sometimes, so it was pretty cool to have a best friend attend the same school. Sometimes Tasha's mom would pick me up or I would ride on the yellow bus to go to school. Either was cool, because I refused to being seen dropped off in Grams green buggy machine she called a car. "Hey girl, what's up?" Tash asked. "Nothing, just upset that my weekend was boring and I'm starting to think about my mom again," I answered.

"Well, let me tell you what I did over the weekend," she said. Captured by her enthusiasm, I asked her what, and she went on to tell me her 16-year-old cousin came over and let her hit a puff of her joint. She claimed it set her on fire and made her giggle all night. She said it was the best night of her life. "Shey, you should have been there. I mean I was blew back." I couldn't believe my ears, even though I shouldn't have been shocked by anything she did. Tash was my best friend, but she was also fast, fast, fast.

We were in Junior High and she was already introduced to the red light district of sin run wild. As I was talking to Tash, I noticed Eric Black looking at me. Tash said, "ooooh, I see you looking at Eric." I ignored her and acted like she was making something out of nothing. Tash immediately dragged me over to where Eric was standing.

"Eric, this is my girl Sheyla, Sheyla this is Eric." How embarrassing. Eric was a kid that all the girls liked. He was tall and dangerous, just like I like 'em. He got kicked out of class everyday. Eric wore Levi's and a silk shirt with a matching handkerchief that hung out of his pants back pocket almost daily. It was only the beginning of winter and he wore a Nanny Goat coat, which was the freshest coat to wear at the time.

He was well dressed and always having crazy cash in his pockets. I kinda believed he sold drugs with his brotha's. Even though we were in the same grade, he was almost two years older than we were. This kid was the bomb. Suddenly, the gym teacher blew the whistle and we all had to sit in our assigned spots on the gym floor. I couldn't keep my eyes off of Eric. He knew I was checkin' him out because he continued to glance at me with this confident stare. Before hitting the showers, we had to put up our equipment. As I was heading to put up the jump rope, Eric kissed me on the cheek. "It's more that comes with that," he whispered. Man, he had to have noticed my embarrassed puzzled look, I mean what did he mean. As he exited out the gym, I fell into a daze. "Shey, Shey, what did he say?" Tash asked anxiously. "Nothing, nothing at all," I responded with a puzzled stare.

That small kiss on the cheek had me in great anticipation of what was to come. I never considered myself to be fast, but living with my grandmother made me second guess everything. With her religion and all, anyone would have second guessed their innocence. I went home wondering how would I react if he French kissed me. I was preparing for the unexpected. Looking at all the different shows that came on television, I was nervous about my lack of kissing experience and so I taught myself. Kissing someone wasn't anything I had ever done before, so I started to practice using my tongue and massaging the back of my hand to imitate a real kiss. "Girl, what in the world are you doing?" Grams blurted out, lowering her alto voice to tenor. Immediately I jumped up, my skin instantly flushed in red. "What? I ain't doing nothin."

"Yeah, nothing better be what you were doing," she said as she went to her room.

Looking forward to the next day, I couldn't wait to step foot in the door, Golightly Educational Center. I was starting to adjust to my new school. Eric had it going on and I was caught up in the moment. Finally, there he was. "Hey Eric." "What's up girl?" Blushing as usual, I asked him what he meant by his little remark in gym class the previous day. He said that he was letting me know he was going to make me feel like a woman. My stomach felt like a wave from the sea shifted from side to side, causing the need to use the bathroom. I became confused.

Did I want him to talk to me that way? Am I ready to feel that way? What's involved with what he was declaring to do to me? "Meet me on the playground after school," he said, but 3:15 wasn't coming fast enough at least it seemed to move slower than usual. The bell wrung like a thunder announcing the end of the school day. I waited so I wouldn't seem like I was pressed to see Eric.

There he was, standing there with his baseball cap pulled over his eyes. "I thought you'd chicken out," he said. "Boy, if anything, I didn't expect you to be here," I answered. He immediately grabbed me and kissed my lips softly. I started to close my eyes and suddenly he forced his tongue in my mouth. I had to open my eyes to see what was taking place.

Slowly I felt him pulling my shirt out of my pants. He started slivering his fingers down my panties. "I'm going to take you there," he said. Oh no! I might have acted grown, but I wasn't that kind of girl. On top of all that, I was too scared to go that far with any boy. "Stop Eric, please stop," I softly whispered. "Girl you want it, you know you do," softly speaking in a mesmerizing voice. I pushed him away and took two steps back. "Boy, I don't know what you thought, you nasty!"

"Shey, you ain't nothing but a little girl, wasting my time. I'm out!" After saying that, he walked away looking at me like I had spit in his face or something. Walking to the bus stop, I saw Tash. "Girl, you're walking like someone took something from you." "Tash, your boy Eric tried to touch me down there," I said. "Ont oon, oh no he didn't. Well did you let him?" Tash responded inquisitively. "Tash, I said he tried, and no I wouldn't go that far."

Tash was looking like, what was the big deal. I had to ask her had she ever been touched down there. She said, "Sheyla, I've gone further than that. Anyways you the biggest attention seeker in the world. He's showing you a lot of attention, so you better holla at Eric, girls all over the school would love to be in your place." Again, nothing Tash said shocked me, she always had secrets and surprises jumping out of the closet. I see why my grandmother wouldn't let her come over to hang out with me. Grams would always say, "something 'bout that Latasha just ain't right."

Going home, all I thought about was Eric. Maybe I should have let him take a visit to my innocence. Tash was kinda right, all the girls did talk about Eric. He was the man at school and I liked him a lot, well at least I thought I did.

It was the weekend and I wasn't myself. I felt like I was going into another level of my life. This level consisted of decisions, developing me into a young woman. I was so young, but life was moving so fast and I wanted to keep up. "Baby, what's wrong, you've been moping around the house all day?" Grams asked. "Nothing, I'm just missing my mom," I said as a quick response before she could interrogate me. Grams gave me a hug and walked out of my room.

I wasn't lying, I really missed my mother, but it was much more than that bothering me. Twelve years old and I'm thinking about being with a boy. I felt like I was letting my grandmother down and was letting Tash influence me. I really was into this Eric kid though. He made me nervous, yet he excited me, which intensified my desire for him. While caught up in my thoughts, Grams yelled out, "Hey Shey, come with me. I'm going with Mrs. Caroline to watch Marcus play basketball."

Well, it was a chance for me to get out of the house. Plus, the way Marcus talked about basketball the last time I saw him intrigued me into wanting to see if he could live up to his own hype. We were running a little behind schedule, so when we arrived there were already a lot of parents at the game. It was cute, because the cheerleading team was made up of girls that were my age dressed in little skirts with matching pom-poms. They cheered as the basketball team was announced. Cheering definitely set the tone for the atmosphere; it was off the hook. I found myself somewhat engrossed in the excitement. We had to stand for a while, 'cause we had gotten to the game a little late; an opening in the bleachers didn't occur until almost halftime.

"Marcuuss, Stuuunson," the announcer yelled with a thunderous sound. Looking at Marcus out there with those big kids was crazy. I was thinking this puny kid is too small to be playing with these big boys. The Falcons were part of the Detroit Police Athletic League (P.A.L.,) and this was the 14 years and under team. Marcus was only twelve and he was starting. Looking at Marcus play made me appreciate how his name could be Stun. He was killing those older kids. I was impressed or shall I say stunned. For a kid to play that well, he had to think, drink, and sleep basketball.

Retraced

The parents on the opposing team were screaming to take him out the game. As he dribbled up the court, the score was 58 to 60; the Falcons were down by two and Marcus had the ball. He slowly glanced at the crowd and got a peep of me cheering him on. When our eyes met, I could tell he was shocked to see me so enthused; his smile said it all. There were 10 seconds left on the game clock. Marcus started yelling "clear out, clear out." Parents continued to scream, "Trap Stun, trap Stun!" Marcus immediately pulled up and shot a jump shot from the three point line. *Swoosh*. The ball went in and the Falcons won the game. Most of the crowd dashed to the floor in exhilaration.

"Hey Marcus, or should I say Stun."

"That shot was for you," he responded with a big grin on his face. He was so proud of himself, I thought it was cute. Mrs. Caroline consumed with joy smiled a smile that bulged through her cheekbones. She just hugged him and kissed him, and then she asked me what I thought of the game. "It was okay." Marcus thought he was the man, so this was my way of bringing him down a notch. "My baby is good," Mrs. Caroline said.

"Hey Sheyla, I'm having a birthday party in two weeks right before New Years. Ask can you come," Marcus said. "Grams can I go to the birthday party?" I asked. Grams was cool with it, she trusted Mrs. Caroline, so going over Marcus's house wasn't a problem at all. Marcus told me he was going to have some of his boys that he plays basketball with come over and he asked me to invite some of my friends too.

Marcus's Gig

It was cool to get out the house, but later that night I continued to think about Eric Black. He simply wouldn't leave my mind. Sunday night I picked out my finest clothes in preparation for the next school day. I was going to impress Eric and get him to forget that little embarrassing episode at the playground. School began and ended with Eric being nowhere in sight. I continued to look for him the whole week, but nothing. He was nowhere to be found. I started wondering if he'd gotten himself into trouble, or was he so upset with me that he decided to drop out of school. Whatever the case, I was miserable. Thoughts wouldn't flow right and school became an immediate bore. Another week passed without a glance of the best looking boy in the school. Tash tried to cheer me up, but I was ready to be with this boy. I felt myself caught in a war of right and wrong, and wrong was winning.

Even though I knew my Grams, God, and whoever else would be disappointed in my desire, I had gotten to the point where it didn't matter. My heart became cold towards things that I once looked at as being moral. What was going on? I hadn't done anything that was worth mentioning, yet I felt this power of undeveloped womanhood growing daily. I was mentally and physically maturing at a rapid rate, accelerating my drive.

My new found attitude had begun to take hold of my clothing. Things were tighter, smaller, and my style wasn't as innocent as it had been. Grams refused to buy me anything that looked too mature, but I knew how to spice things up and could make it work, thanks to, you guessed it, Tash.

Saturday came around and it was time for me and Grams to go to Marcus' birthday party. I was kind of excited to go because Marcus asked me to invite some of my friends. I had a liking to doing hair, often times experimenting on myself. I buffed my long flowing hair with curls, giving me a more mature look and was ready to hang out. I invited two girls from my school and of course my girl Tasha. Wherever she went, she became the life of the party. Grams wasn't too pleased with Tash coming along, but showing me mercy, she picked Tash up anyway. Grams believed with her presence at the party, nothing terrible could happen. Entering the party, I realized it wasn't the kind of party I was expecting. No one was dancing and the music they were playing was gospel music. Man, this was wacked, I looked at Tash and her expression said it all.

Mrs. Caroline greeted us and told us to go to the basement where everyone was. There were some girls mingling, but mostly boys. When we walked in, all the boys turned, staring at me-of-course and Tash, Tre, and Michelle. I took off my rubberband holding my long hair in a ponytail allowing my hair to flow down my shoulders, knowing it would catch the attention of all the onlookers. I had a tap on my shoulder, so I looked to see who it was. On the spot, my eyes looked into his eyes where we locked in a daze. It was Eric. My legs felt like stilts trying to hold up a heavy house, my tongue went dry and my words were stuck. "Wassup," he said. "You," I paused. "And where have you been?" I asked.

"I was helping my brotha's out with some family bizness, ya know," Eric said with a voice slightly above a whisper. "What family business?" He quietly responded,

"Nothin' of importance. So Shey, how do you know Stun?"

"Stun! Oh yeah, you mean Marcus. Marcus is like a little brotha. My Grams is real cool with his grandmother," I answered. Eric was looking and smelling good. He had a fresh fade and a new diamond earring in his ear. He acted differently this day too; he was real calm and mellow. He said he didn't mean to push me too far on the playground. I let him know it wasn't a problem and that he could have a second chance if he wanted it. "Hey, let's go out back for some privacy," Eric said.

Going to the backyard brought on nervous feelings again, I mean, what would he try next? Before we sat down on the bench, Eric grabbed my arm and stroked my hair like a man pets his dog. "It's nice to see you again." His voice, his smile had me in a zone of Ericism. After staring in my eyes, he kissed me, making his tongue massage mine. Practicing kissing my hand paid off after all. He complimented me on the kiss. I totally forgot where I was. Grams, Mrs. Caroline and the other kids were all non-existent; I was in another world.

Out of the blue, a disapproving face appeared. "What's up E.B., what's up Shey," Marcus said with a light voice. He looked like he was about to cry. My heart understood, yet I had mixed emotions, because I felt I didn't owe Marcus an explanation, but at the same time, I didn't want my Grams to find out.

"Shey, your grandmother was looking for you, so I decided to find you," Marcus' voice muttered with obvious disappointment. The party for me kind of ended because of my embarrassment. My interest was gone and I was ready to go. As the party continued, I stared and blushed at Eric from afar. He knew what was going through my mind. My thoughts were totally on finishing what we started. Before the party ended, one of Eric's brothers, Ja'Ron picked him up. Eric introduced us and off the bat I saw the resemblance. His brother was even cuter and looked to only be a year or two older than he was. Before Eric left, he whispered in my ear, "I can't wait to see you Monday."

Grams, my three friends and I decided to stay back and help Mrs. Caroline clean up, one of Marcus's friends also helped. I didn't know his name, but he looked familiar. Marcus did everything in his power to avoid me. It was an awkward situation, but I was kind of glad, because I didn't feel like explaining myself. The night ended with a very dry goodbye between Marcus and I. "Hey Shey, what's up with the little munchkin over there," Tash asked. "Girl, he has a crush on me and he saw me and Eric kickin it."

"Shey, he's a busta, a little momma's boy," Tash whispered in my ear. We laughed and gave each other a high five.

Love at First Sight
MARCUS......

✤

As I stared at the Polaroid, I couldn't help but feel a fervent craze for the reflection of perfection in the figure. I'll never forget the very first time I met her. Her picture didn't do her justice because her face was even more radiant than I expected. It was obvious I fell for her well before I really knew her. Sheyla. When my grandmother introduced me to her, I was nervous and so I put on the *macho, I'm the man* introduction. "My boys call me Stun" slipped out of my mouth before I could catch it. What was she thinking? I mean I had to have looked like a straight up mark busta.

The night continued and I calmed down realizing she was good people. Our conversation was thought stimulating, equally as impressive as her physical beauty; we clicked. I nearly opened up to her to tell her about why I was living with my grandmother. I used to live in the Brewster Projects on the eastside of Detroit with my mom, well before Sheyla had moved in the projects with her grandmother. She started selling drugs for her boyfriend, Quatrel, the neighborhood big shot. Quatrel got caught up in a bad drug deal and ran off with money that he was fronted. Someone looking for revenge couldn't find him and decided to kill my mom instead. She was shot 10 times in her head. Somehow a hysterical little nine year old wasn't viewed as a good witness, so the police never investigated the murder with the information I gave them. I supplied a good description and no action was ever taken. Hiding behind the couch, I watched it happen. Everything was vividly clear. Unfortunately many murders in the projects went unsolved. People started unconfirmed rumors that some guy named Terry Clemons, nicknamed T.C. murdered her. Family members told me to shut my mouth before he found out there was a witness and he came after me. Seeing the murder was devastating. It happened 2 ½ years prior to me meeting Sheyla, and it still bothered me terribly. I had never discussed it with anyone outside of the family, yet Sheyla's beauty almost caused me to open up to her hoping for empathy.

My grandmother and I decided to keep family business confidential because she believed that my mother's situation would continually traumatize me and potentially cause people to perceive me negatively. So, I became less talkative than your normal 12 year old kid. Before I came to live with my grandmother, the previous years consisted of me trying to find a home. I stayed in foster homes at cousins and with my mother friends who couldn't afford to keep me, so my grandmother decided to make the sacrifice and take me in. I owe her so much. After my mom died, I felt unloved, confused and became very depressed; then came my hero, Grandma Caroline.

Very young and dealing with problems that most adults couldn't handle, the one thing that kept me sane was basketball. The game became my best friend. I usually played ball with older kids and quite often played better. The basketball court was my world; I controlled it and the people on it. I became a very confident hooper.

Dope dealers around the neighborhood recruited players like me to play against other hoods. They would gamble on the games for weekend fun and neighborhood bragging rights. One day we played this team from the North Inn. The team was sponsored by Tim Black and two of his brothers played for him. Ja'Ron and Eric. Ja'Ron could play a little, but he was all talk and mostly on a thugged out kick. Eric was nice on the court, he had skills, but was a terrible student. The neighborhood knew he had flunked a couple of times and wasn't interested in playing organized sports. I believe this is what pushed him to sell drugs with his brothers. He was cool and we were good friends. I often played basketball against him and others from their neighborhood, but for some strange reason his brother Ja'Ron didn't like me. Maybe it was because he was a show off and every time I played against him, I embarrassed him at least that's the only conclusion I could come up with for him not liking me.

Basketball and drugs were the only ways out of the gutter and I wasn't choosing the path that could have ended my life early like my mother's. So I practiced day and night. The neighbors would ask me to put the ball up because bouncing the ball on the pavement late at night irritated them. It didn't bother me because I was a determined young man. National Basketball Association (NBA.), here I come.

Looking at how the older kids were ending up and the future of some of the younger ones, life wasn't going to consume me and make me into a stereotypical young thug. Fitting in with the wild crowd wasn't my thing. My boys called me a church boy, because Grandma made me go to church every Sunday. "Church boy, church boy," is what they would sing, with laughs following. To them going to church made me weak. My opinion of myself was quite different. I mean, I saw all the harsh realities that being a gangster had to offer. I compared gangsterism to doctors, lawyers, teachers, business owners, and of course athletes and there wasn't a comparison. Most of my friends' brothers, dads, cousins, and any other male that we associated with usually had a criminal record or were dead. My life meant so much more and I had to return my grandmother's gift of saving me from being a foster kid. I often asked myself what would have happened to me without my grandmother and my homeboy Dannie.

Dannie was my boy. We've played basketball together since the age of seven. He was the silliest guy you could meet. He was the only true stable person in my life, besides grandma Caroline. Neither of us had siblings, so we weren't just best friends, we were brothers. One day I told him about Sheyla, because he went to the same school she did and he told me to watch out for her because she hung around a girl named Tasha. Supposedly Tasha was looked at as a fast, troubled girl that was very experienced in life. He called her a girl version of Eric Black. "Those kinda girls don't pay attention to cats like us. I've been trying to get with Tasha forever and she told me I was a little boy. And dawg, we're the same age," Dannie told me on the phone laughing. He continued to tell me that Sheyla didn't know him because she and her girls only hung out with the rowdy crew. Nothing he said mattered, because I was going to make Sheyla mine straight up like Alfalfa fought for Darla on The Little Rascals. She was a challenge.

It was a week before we played one of our biggest P.A.L. basketball games; both teams were undefeated and we were fighting for the number one spot in our division. Man, I was excited. This game positioned me against one of the best point guards in our age group, Lester Vains, so I figured this game would be a way to show off and get Shey's attention.

I asked my grandmother to invite Ms. Patron and Sheyla to my game. Days leading up to the big game, I didn't get a feel from my grandma that Sheyla and her grandmother would show up, my focus shifted directly on the game and Lester Vains. I heard so much about him and just playing against him would help me assess where I really was as a basketball player. I mean there was a lot of hype around my name; in fact many high school coaches started coming to the games trying to recruit me to their schools, but my grandmother always kept me level headed though and I wasn't getting caught up in the hype. Lester had the same hype surrounding his name. He was older, taller, bigger and had more to prove than I did. Again, I welcomed challenges.

Whenever I was dealing with anything major or stressful, I'd get a headache; this time was no different than any other because my head was grinding. Grandma said she was going to get me checked out because my headaches were serious, sometimes to the point of me vomiting.

Nothing was going to prevent me from winning this game. Saturday came around and it was game time. Early that morning I took a dump in the toilet, along with my headaches, this was a ritual before every big game. My nerves always got the best of me. Walking into the gym, I noticed all the parents, kids from all kind of neighborhoods, and high school coaches whose faces were familiar. No sign of Sheyla. Oh well, I had to take care of business anyhow. Lester and I met at half court and shook hands. The referee tossed the ball up and we were off. The game was very exciting and intense. The first play began with Lester coming down launching one from three all bottoms. He scored on the next two possessions and they led 7 to nothing. Before I knew it, they had put on a half court press and the score was 18 to 4. Now, could I let that happen? Of course not. I shot and made three straight three pointers and now the crowd was really into it. The fans were getting the show that they were expecting. My boy Dannie was playing his heart out too. He wasn't highly touted, but cats had to respect his game because he could rain the three point shot like nobody's business. He helped keep us in the game. By the time the third quarter began, the score was tied. I was walking the ball up court and that's when I heard a familiar voice screaming, it was Shey.

Man, it was time to let Lester and his team, the Bulldogs have it. The score was tied with 40 seconds remaining in the fourth quarter. Lester had the ball. I scored 24 points, 10 assists and was having a great game. Earlier in the game, I noticed that Lester had a tendency. His eyes would widen and his lips would twitch before making a hard drive to the left. One thing that separated me from a lot of players was that I noticed every thing about a player. I watched for patterns, studied plays, and simply did whatever I could to gain the edge on an opponent. Lester's eyes widened, then his lip twitched and I stopped him from going to his favorite spot. He had to pass the ball to his teammate; his teammate shot and made the basket.

Immediately our coach called a time out. Coach said let's run our favorite play.

Everyone in the gym knew the play. Get Stun the ball. Five seconds was left on the clock and Lester's team was winning by two points. I got the ball at half court. I took a quick peep in the crowd, noticing Sheyla hysterically cheering our team on. I gave a hard fake to the left and did a quick Isiah Thomas crossover. One defender stepped up to help Lester, but I drove past him, faked a pass to Dannie and pulled at the three-point line. Bottoms. All nets. The shot went in and we won the game. Everyone came running on the court. My Grandma was so proud of me. It was like it was her first time watching me play and she could see why basketball was so important to me. It took me away from the pains and struggles I dealt with on the regular.

"My baby is good, give me a hug boy," Grandma said with a tear in her eyes. Coaches came up to me, but I ignored them, because there were only two people I wanted to talk to before they left. I quickly ran up to Lester to congratulate him on a great game. Even though I ended up winning the battle, I respected what this kid could do on the court. We gave each other dap and he said, "I'm sure we'll meet up in high school or may even play summer league together."

While talking to him, I felt someone poking me in the back. Turning around, I noticed Shey standing there with a smile. She gave me a big hug. My Grandmother asked her what she thought about the game and she responded sarcastically of course. At this point, I thought I had won her over. Man, was I dumb. My thirteenth birthday was coming up, and I felt like this was a chance to spend quality time with my dream girl, so I invited her.

Going to school the following week after the big game was crazy. Teachers had heard about the game and they were congratulating me on my performance. All of a sudden I was the talk of the school. I guess this was a taste of what was to come cause people in Detroit really loved basketball.

We didn't have our own basketball team, yet the girls were treating me like they were at the game. Man, this was weird because I was the smallest kid in the school. Growing up, I had the little man's complex, but basketball changed all. "Hey Stun, what did you get on the Math test," Gina spoke trying to spark a conversation. This girl Gina was real cute. All of the fella's liked her. She was tight, but again I had my eyes on higher ground, Sheyla. Gina was nice, but she was typical. I wasn't feeling her. I mean, just the previous week I spoke to her and she didn't even acknowledge my existence.

Higher Ground

Everyone was riding this path to destruction and at a young age I was looking for something that was real. I couldn't put my finger on it, but I knew life had much more than what I could see or perceive. Every night I was having dreams. There was one dream that I couldn't get out of my head. This angel comes down from the heavens confronting me by blowing words and wind into my mouth. All of a sudden I fall out and the words come out of me without me opening my mouth, while I'm laying down, touching strangers and loved ones. Every time I dream I'm visited by the angel, the dream is a little different but not by much. Whatever it meant, it had me trippin'. Sharing this with anyone would label me a lunatic and I wasn't down with that. This dream had me continually thinking about heaven and God. I was confused about so many things and this God thing had me uncertain. Was God really real? That night I prayed.

Hey Lord,

How are you? Who are you? Where are you? My life has had so many bad turns, what is the purpose of my life? I'm praying to find these things out because I want to be a good person and do the world some good. Please help me! I have so many dreams, like playing in the N.B.A., buying my grandmother a beautiful house and marrying a girl that's real. Oh, Lord, thanks for lettin' me meet Sheyla, 'cause I see a lot of me in her. Just talkin' to her, it's like she needs someone to protect her. And Lord I'm up for it, I promise. And you know I keep my promises. Well, I know I'm asking for a lot, but I want to really get to know you for who you are.

In God's name,
Amen.

Well this was the only way to state my case because I didn't know if there was a format, and if so, what was it? Praying wasn't anything I was used to, but this night I felt an urge to do it.

Some Surprise

It was two days before my birthday party and I needed to pick out my best clothes. Shey and her girls were coming over and I knew they were going to set it off. It was imperative that I did the same. I picked out my Girbaud Jeans, which were big enough to fit two of me in. The matching Girbaud shirt had me looking tight. My grandmother took me down town to Alantis to get the fresh fade; I was fly.

"Yo, Dannie, we're picking you up in 30 minutes to help us set-up for tonight. Are you ready?" I asked over the phone.

"Yeah, dawg, come through," he answered. I knew Dannie was very excited about my party because he was anticipating Tasha being there. He wanted another go at trying to holla. There was only one problem, Grandma wanted to play church music and didn't want, well, how did she say it, "I don't want that worldly music in my house." She was trippin! "Grandma, it doesn't have to be rap or vulgar, but come on. We're kids, I'll be the joke of the neighborhood, " I begged. She finally gave in and compromised.

She let us choose some songs that didn't talk about sex or drugs. The compromise was to play both music styles. My thought was how will we find a song without those key elements. We had some of the prettiest girls in the 'D' coming over. Well, right when the party was about to start, Dannie and I didn't have enough soda, plus I wanted to be the focal point of my party, so we decided to be late.

We went to the store up the street. Before returning to the party, we bought some gum and peppermints. We were all prepared to talk to the girls and have us a girlfriend by the end of the night. On our way back to the party, we were discussing some of our techniques and what we were going to say. "Tasha, I know you really don't know me, but I've been watching you for a while and I finally got the heart to holla at you," Dannie said with confidence.

"Dannie man, you sound like a stalker, I've been watching you for a while; you are straight sounding desperate," I said. We laughed trying to calm down from the anticipation of the girls coming over. Sheyla's heart was an opponent that I was willing to take on. I compared it to basketball; any obstacle in hoops was conquered through dedication and persistency. My heart was set on winning Shey's affection.

When I hit the door, I saw Grandma talking to Mrs. Patron. This meant that Sheyla wasn't too far behind. Going to the back, I heard Stevie Wonder's Ribbon in the Sky playing on the radio. I figured I was just in time to ask that special girl to dance. She was nowhere in sight. "Sheyla, Sheyla, come here please," her grandmother calling for her whereabouts. She wasn't in the basement or living room, so I decided to look in the backyard. From afar I could see Sheyla was with a boy. The closer I got to where they were, I noticed she's passionately kissing my boy Eric Black. Heartache tore through my soul. Devastation wasn't the word, I felt inwardly dead!

My mouth dropped. They were so involved in their kiss; they didn't notice I was watching. The only thing I could do was to greet them both. What was she doing? This was my party; she knew how I felt about her. She hurt me and looking at her, she had no regrets. I could deal with her talking to someone else, but why did she have to be all up in my face wit it.

As the night ended, Shey and Tasha were whispering and I knew it was something about me. Lord knows I couldn't wait for this nightmare to be over. When Sheyla left, Dannie gave me a pound and put his right arm around my neck, "Stun, I ain't trying to hurt your feelings, but 'ole girl called you a busta and then had the audacity to laugh at you. Dawg, you are a hooper. Why deal with a girl like that? When you make it to the league, you'll have females beggin' to be your girl." Dannie always knew how to cheer me up, but this time it didn't work.

Thou Sayeth Go!

A week went by and it was time for church. Our church had a guest speaker, Prophet Louis. He started to prophesy and tell people what God wanted to do in their lives. Man, while I was wishing for him to call me up, he noticed me. "Young man come up front," he said. Not sure he was talking to me, I looked all around, then pointed to myself, "Yes you young man."

"God has given you a vision that shall come to pass. Stay strong. He said that your heart longs for him and you want to get to know him. You shall touch many hearts in an unconventional way. Read the Bible, says God almighty. I will visit you when you least expect it. Quit worrying about this and that, just trust Me. I am dealing with you in your dreams." Prophet Louis continued, but it was quite amazing to hear someone state things that were exactly what I needed to hear from God. I wasn't totally convinced this prophecy thing was true, but I was overwhelmed with the possibilities. This was the first time that I had really gotten something good out of church.

Tears filled my eyes, but I held strong and didn't get all emotional. That day had me thinking about my life. What

Retraced

did the future have in store for a kid with issues? Immediately, Sheyla kissing Eric popped in my head again. I picked up the phone to call her and right when someone picked up the phone, I hung up. What could I have said?

Growing Up SHEYLA......

This was the first time I anticipated going to school regularly. I mean the weekends became more of a struggle, because I was bored. Grams felt I was too young to let me catch the bus anywhere, and all of my friends stayed too far away. The morning broke and it was time for Eric's world to begin. Exhilarated about being his girl, I skipped my first hour class to meet him at his. "Hey Eric," I whispered. "What's up girl?" he responded, politely stroking my shoulder. I asked him what he had going on after school. He said he had a few minutes to spare, but had to rush home to help his brothers handle some things. At this point I was very irritated with him. One minute, he's all in to me; the next he's avoiding me. I was confused and wondering what in the world was going on. I decided to avoid our little planned meeting. I went searching for my girl Tasha. She was the one person I could rely on to listen to my problems. I got so caught up in talking to her; I didn't realize I had walked her home.

"Shey, how are you going to get home? You missed the big cheese," Tash said. "You're right, what am I going to do? Grams is going to kill me." Tasha always had a solution.

"Girl, your boy Eric doesn't stay too far, I'll walk you over there and ask if one of his brothers can take you home," she replied. It was cool with me. I mean it was a chance to see Eric and get home without Grams suspecting anything.

Eric's house set on the end of a dead end block. Walking up to the house, it was clear it was the epic center of dysfunctional behavior. There were three teenage boys sitting on the porch smoking cigarettes and weed. These young marijuana kings had no shame. The music was loud, filled with profane words and it seemed that the neighbors didn't mind. I'm from the hood, but this block took hoodism to a whole different level.

Kids were playin' basketball on crates, homes were burned down from obvious gang friction, and I was straight-up nervous. Approaching the door, one of the boys on the porch said, "who ya'll here to see?" "Me fool," a voice meeting us at the door. It was Eric. He had this shocked expression on his face. I was expecting a greeting of joy, but his reaction was different. "Tash, why did you bring Shey over here?" He mumbled. "Hey, I don't mean any trouble, but I missed my ride and was hoping my boyfriend could help me out!"

"Look, I didn't mean anything by that," he said. As he reluctantly let us in, I began to understand why he wasn't comfortable with me visiting. His house was unkept. The house was very dark and smelled like weed and pee all mixed into one big disgusting stench. It reminded me of how my house with my moms and T.C. was.

I didn't want to embarrass him any further so I acted as if I hadn't seen anything and gave him a big hug. He smiled, "My brother Ja'Ron has the car and he'll be back soon." "So, where is your mom, I'd like to meet her?" I asked. As soon as I said that, a heavy set lady walked in. You could tell she had just gotten out of bed because her hair was everywhere and she still had pajamas on. "Ma, this Sheyla, Shey this is my mom," Eric introduced us.

One of the boys that was on the porch walked in with a joint in his hand. Eric's mom took the joint out of his hand and puffed it. "Boy, I'm the only one that does the smoking in this house," she said. Man, I felt so embarrassed for Eric. His mom was out cold. "Ms. Black it's nice to finally meet you," I said to defuse the embarrassment I felt for her. "Thanks. Nice to meet you too lil' youngin.' Tasha, this must be yo only friend wit' manna's," she said with a smirk. Talking ghetto trashy, she was the epitome of being set up for failure. How could her sons have a chance in life? I thought my upbringing was foul, but this was off the chaasain.

Eric immediately took my hand and Tash followed us upstairs to his room. Eric slid over clothes on the sheetless bed, revealing stains that had me not wanting to sit down. The bed sat directly across from a television that had a wire hanger cropped on top. "So Eric, What family business did you have to rush home to handle?" I asked. He paused and tried to get off the subject. I got upset because I knew he was hiding something. "Look, if you got another girl, I wish you'd tell me," I said ready to storm out of the house.

"Man, alright! Some boys around the way threatened my brother and I was rollin' out to settle that issue. I got home late, so Ja'Ron and my other brotha's left without me. But there is something I need to tell you." He took a deep breath and continued. "Eric," his mom called interrupting our small talk. "Come get this boy!" Ms. Black walked upstairs holding a newborn baby. "That trifling girl brought little Eric by," his mom said as she handed him the baby and left. Tasha yelled out "Little Eric!" Eric looked disturbed, "Shey, that's what I was trying to tell you, I have a son." I immediately turned red. I couldn't believe that this chump left out this very important family member when telling me about his immediate bloodline ties. "A mom, three brothers, but how could you leave out your own son," I said. I was all in an uproar ready to push the panic alarm, yet I still couldn't drag myself away from his presence. This boy had my mental and my physical, he had me good.

Eric walked towards me and immediately stuck his tongue down my throat. He asked Tasha if she could give us some privacy. Eric laid the baby in his bed and then laid me next to him. He began massaging my thighs and hips; I began to caress his head and back. He sat me up, sparking my hormones into submission. My heart was beating fast and I was excited about being with him.

I relaxed my body across the bed and felt the baby moving. This immediately brought me back to reality. Oh no, I wasn't having it. "Eric I'm sorry, but I can't take a chance of being your next trifling victim as your mom would say." "What?" he responded. Eric looked with an intensity that scared the innocence out of me.

He smacked me and ripped open my shirt. He said I was trippin' again and he knew I really wanted it. I screamed "Get off of me!" Tash came running in the door. "Girl, what's up?" She asked. "Please get me out of here," I hysterically cried out. "Man, Eric, get away from her," Tasha yelled. Tasha threw me her sweater and I put it on. Eric said, "Girl you ain't worth the trouble anyway, let me get my brotha to shoot you to tha crib."

As his brothers pulled up in the car, two of them got out first. Tasha asked Ja'Ron, the brother I recognized from Marcus' party, to take me home. I was surprised he said yes. Ja'Ron dropped Tasha off first. "What's wrong with you?" Ja'Ron asked. I told him nothing was wrong, gave him directions and thanked him for taking me home. The trip home was quiet. I was thinking about the incident the entire ride. Eric, the one I was crazy for, totally just disrespected me. My thoughts were filled with questions about his baby and the mother. I mean, how did Eric treat her?

Love, Rights, and War

❈

The time was 7:00 p.m. and Grams had choir rehearsal, so she was nowhere to be found. I knew I was going to be in big trouble because I was more than two hours late. She was never late for anything dealing with church, so I really didn't expect her to be home.

Ring, Ring, who could this be? I answered the phone and there was a young man's voice on the phone. "What do you want?" thinking it was Eric. "Dang kidd, I'm just calling to see how you were doing. It's me, Stun." Man, it was good to hear a trustworthy voice. "I'm sorry," I responded. "I just had a very rough day." Marcus asked, "What's wrong?" The embarrassment wouldn't allow me to respond. Plus, I didn't want to hear any sarcastic remarks.

I asked him what was up. He said "Sheyla, I just like hearing your voice. I called a few minutes ago, but hung up because I felt dumb calling you, but I just had to."

"What is it Marcus?" I asked. "I couldn't put the vision of you kissing Eric out of my mind. I mean you don't owe me anything, but you know how I feel about you," he said. Man, I wish I could have said I felt the same way, but the truth was he was like a little brotha. No attraction, and too nice for me. I was simply irritated by the thought. Little man Marcus was the complete opposite of what I wanted in a man; cute, hard and gangsta. To be honest, I even thought about trying to patch things up with Eric, but I just couldn't. "Eric, I mean Marcus, let's just be friends alright. Right now is not a good time. Plus, you don't have to worry about me kissing Eric anytime soon."

Of course he wanted to know why, and I ended up telling him what had happened earlier between Eric and I. It was apparent that he was disappointed with the rejection again, but he took it like a man. Marcus made mention that Eric needed to pay for what he had done. I was praying his little puny self wouldn't do anything crazy. Marcus' words were soothing and I enjoyed talking to him. Our conversation continued until I heard keys rattling at the door.

"Marcus, Grams is here and I have to go. Bye." Before I hung up the phone, Marcus slipped in "Look, one day you're going to be my wife." That boy didn't give up. I thought for a second, marriage sounded nice, especially to Treach from Naughty by Nature. He was the man in hip hop at the time. I simply loved his hard, dark and thuggish sexiness. In the midst of me thinking, I heard a loud yell, "Sheyla, bring your little narrow behind down here, right now!"

Grams was upset and I had never heard so much anger in her voice until today. She couldn't believe I missed the bus and how irresponsible I was. I wasn't affected until she started to mention my mother and how I was lost, heading in the same direction as her. Her inconsiderate remarks devastated me, especially not knowing if my mother was dead or not. I knew Grams was mad, but this ate at me and I had to express it. "How in the hell are you talking about my mother like you all perfect or something? Running around praying to a God that don't even answer your prayers." What in the world was I thinking? I couldn't control my anger at this point and I guess I had felt like that for a while. This was my opportunity to let her know and those harsh words flowed like water. "Hell, you actually used the word hell derogatively to me without any regards. You are a very disrespectful little girl. You are on punishment. No television, no phone calls, no nothing and I mean it. Just stay up in your room!" I walked upstairs and really didn't regret what I had just said. She paid no mind to the pain I felt daily. All of a sudden, my door burst open and there she was holding a switch she had ripped off the branch in front of our house. I thought I was too old to get spanked, but she didn't think so. She started wailing on me. I rolled under the bed and stayed there until she left. "Shey, how dare you, how dare you!" Grams yelled as she finally walked out of my room.

The next day Tasha greeted me in school with, "What's up Shey?"

"Everything. Me and Grams got into a big argument and now I'm on punishment. She didn't even tell me for how long." Tasha said it wasn't a big deal because she was always on punishment. It never stopped her from doing her dirt. I was beginning to understand Tash a little more. I mean, how can people expect us to be little girls when we've encountered and experienced women problems. I really started to feel her. I asked Tasha did she talk to anyone about my little incident with Eric and she said she hadn't. I still felt like people knew and I was avoiding Eric at all cost.

Living with Grams became unbearable for the both of us. She never apologized for insulting my mother and I never apologized for yelling at her. Punishment was foul. She lived up to her strict rules and made sure I was in church everyday she went. This was usually three times a week. I couldn't wait to get old enough to leave this torment.

One day, Tasha ran up to me in school telling me about a surprise party her mom was throwing for her 17 year old cousin Jackie. Jackie was graduating from high school and she was going off to college in Pennsylvania. Of course

Tash wanted me to go, but I knew Grams wasn't having it. "Grams, can I go to Tasha cousin's graduation celebration," I asked. "Absolutely not," she said making her eyebrows meet in the center of her head. Weeks passed since the incident between she and I and she was still trippin'. The party was in two days and Tasha told me everyone who was going to be at the gig. This was going to be a pretty cool party. Tasha and her older cousin were very close, so I was very excited about the potential of an older crowd attending. I decided I was going to this party, no matter what!

The night of the party I pretended to go to bed. Grams slept hard and this night was no different. She was snoring. The sound was loud enough to wake up the dead. I figured it was around 9 p.m. and my goal was to leave out and then sneak back in without her knowing anything. I double checked her room before I made my escape.

Everything was safe and I was ready. I called Tasha and her cousin Jackie met me a block away from our section of the projects to pick me up. We got to the party and it was on. It seemed like everyone that was anyone was there. Eric's older brother, Ja'Ron, all the local drug dealers, and of course the sleaziest sack chasers in the area. Oh yeah, there were five other girls from our crew with us. This was what I was waiting for, socializing with older boys, straight up thugs and hardcore gangsta's.

The party was hyped, but it was clear who was getting all the attention, Jackie and her sleazy crew. Jackie took some of her girls to the back room. A few of the men followed. Tash and I wanted to see what was going on. We cracked open the closed door. Jackie was standing on the table dancing, taking off her blouse. The other girls were dancing on top of the boys as they continued to stuff dollars down their panties. "Girl look at all that money they gettin'," Tasha said. Excited, Tash leaned against the door. "Who is that?" One of the guys yelled, so we ran to where the rest of the crowd was. Walking through the smoke filled room, we saw a few sordid looking girls letting guys feel all over their bodies. I also noticed that the boys who didn't have on fly gear, or weren't flashing big knots of cash didn't get much attention. As the sounds cranked louder and louder, my conversations ended and I sat back and monitored the scene. It was quite noticeable how the women were the ones in complete control, using their assets to manipulate the situation. I decided then and right then that I wanted to do the same thing one day. Just controlling men, having them melt in my hands was regulating my thoughts at the moment. Tash was more caught up on what was happening in the back room. "Shey, all that money and just fa dancin'," she pondered out loud. Out of the blue, we heard a lot of commotion and arguments going on upstairs. Next, all you heard, boom, bla, bla, boom. Some dude fell down the stairs or should I say was thrown. "I'll be back," the dude said. I watched the guy out the door then turned in Tasha's direction, "Yo Tash, I need to be on my way home."

"Girl, what are you worried 'bout. Ain't nothin 'bout to happen."

Thirty minutes went by and all you heard was "Open up, it's the police." Low and behold, the kid who was kicked down the stairs was snitching to the police about there being dope in the house and told them he was robbed and beat. "D'are they go, right d'are," he said pointing to some scary looking young guys standing right in front of me. He also mentioned that there were minors smoking weed and drinking in the house. The police immediately asked for everyone to show I.D. I'm the first one they asked. I told them I was 18 and they immediately started shutting down the party. "Okay everyone lets go. It's apparent we have minors in the house and it's late." It was certain the officers didn't believe a word I said. He asked if my mother knew I was out so late on a school night. I started to lie, but what was the use, plus I didn't want Grams to get in trouble for my foolishness. Since I stayed the farthest from the party, the cops escorted me home. They knocked on the door, rung the bell, and finally Grams came staggering half asleep to the door. "Yes," she said. "It's the police," one of the officer's responded. She opened the door and saw me. Her eyes almost popped out of her head, and all I saw was fire in her eyes.

The entire time the police officer was explaining the situation, Grams, with her arms folded was staring right through me. When I stepped in the house, she immediately smacked me and told me to go upstairs and never to come out. "Girl I don't have words that can explain my disappointment, my disgust, and embarrassment. What are you trying to do to me?" After the police left, she walked upstairs, passing my room. All through the night I heard her crying and praying to God. "Lord, what have I done wrong? I try, I promise you, I try." She was loud with no shame. It was keeping me up, so I was irritated with her inability to control her emotions. I was thinking at the time that she needed to just deal with the situation, do whatever she was going to do to me and be true to it. Why cry and get all hysterical. I honestly believed that she had brought this mess on herself. Thinking about my mother's situation, the rape, the emotional issues, and her having me as a result of the rape, Grams could have been more empathetic. No, oh no, Grams was caught up on some ole' self righteous garbage, as if she'd done everything right.

The Teenage Years

The school year was coming to an end. Grams and I really weren't seeing eye to eye. I began to become more rebellious and it got to the point where nothing including counseling, punishment, nor church was doing me any good. I had so much anger built up and didn't know how to release it any other way but through rebellion.

Going to school was a getaway from the warden and my house, which I called prison. I often felt relieved going to school. My grades were decent, but my behavior was off the hook. One day I was kicked out of class and sent in the hallway for talking during instruction time. While in the hallway, I had a strange encounter with Eric. We hadn't talked in weeks, straight up ignoring each other, but this day he approached me with something obviously on his mind.

"Girl, look at my eye, next time you want me to beat down somebody, just ask me. If Marcus wasn't my boy, I probably would have killed that little nigga," he said. "What are you talking about?" I asked. "Your boy fronted on me about the last little situation you and I had, like he was your daddy or somethin." Holding back my grin, I tried to imagine the scene, "He did what?" Irritably, Eric said, "You know exactly what happened. You set it up and if it ever happens again, I'm taking it out on you."

Man, what was Marcus thinking about. I mean he could have gotten hurt. Dumb move on his part, but I thought it was kinda cute too. I couldn't wait to get home and ask him what happened. In the meantime, the bell rung and it was time to transition to a different class. Tasha came out and I had to tell my girl what happened. She couldn't believe what she was hearing. "You mean, puny, little man got some heart, huh. Shey you got it going on. Boys are fighting over you like you are a star or something. He really, really likes you, especially trying to fight Eric, one of the hardest playas we know." I had to tell her about Eric's eye. It was big, purple and protruding. Marcus must have hit him good. Me and Tash couldn't get enough of this story. When school let out we saw Eric at a glance and Tasha said, "girl, Marcus did that to his eye, dang!" Yeah, I definitely had to go home and get the whole scoop from my little hero.

As I hit the door, Grams said "Put your books up, we're going over Mrs. Caroline's house." Good, because I was about to sneak on the phone and call Marcus anyways. This was the first time I was really pressed to see Marcus, or should I say Stun. As soon as we walked in the door, Mrs. Caroline asked my Grams to come look at her Marcus's face. Uh, ooh, I thought. I was wondering if she knew the fight happened as a result her grandson's crush on me. Man, this could spell major trouble. I mean, me getting a good friend hurt over the mess that I was involved in, Grams could have murdered me or just send me away.

After losing her daughter, it was obvious Mrs. Caroline was overly protective of Marcus. She kept talking about getting the police involved, taking him to the hospital, and moving him away. "I swear, I lost one child to these crazy streets in Detroit. I refuse to lose another one." She was trippin'. As I stepped into the room, I noticed Marcus holding a pack of ice over his eye. "What's up slugger?" I whispered. He smirked, "Chillin'."

My Grams started questioning Mrs. Caroline about what happened. Mrs. Caroline told her that Marcus said it had something to do with basketball, but he wouldn't elaborate. Mrs. Caroline and my Grams were so much alike. Both were nice looking for their age, God-fearing, and overly dramatic. Marcus got my attention and immediately gestured me to go downstairs with him. Before we hit the last step, questions started pouring out of my mouth. "How did it start?" "Why did you fight him?" "Who won?"

"Wooooaaa girl, hold your horses." I only fought him because of what he did to you." I told him he was crazy. Flattery wasn't the word, but I was hyped about how he could do this for me, even though I hadn't treated him the best. All of a sudden I had a flash back and began feeling like the girls at Tasha's cousin's party. With a little flirtation, you can get a guy to do anything. I thought the whole thing was so endearing. I had to reward him with a kiss. I grabbed the back of his head and gave him a peck on the forehead.

"Thanks. That kiss reminds me of how my grandmother kisses me. How cute." I couldn't do anything but laugh. "So, are you off your punishment?" He asked. "Naw, not really, grams just hasn't been as strict. It's like she's starting to give up on me," I said. Marcus had this look in his eyes like why can't I just get it right? There was no way for him to understand. Me understanding me was difficult, so I knew I couldn't explain it to him. "But enough of this small talk, tell me everything," I emphatically asked him. After asking me where I wanted him to start, his story went like this.

After their weekend basketball-pick up game at the Belmont Center, Marcus approached Eric. "Hey man, I heard about Shey's visit to yo crib." "Yeah dawg, she came over looking tight. I had to try to hit that," Eric

Retraced

said smiling. He continued to tell and demonstrate how he passionately kissed me and how I was moaning his name Eric, Eric, please. "Stun, I started massaging her breast and whispering in her ear. She couldn't resist the mack down I put on her. I knew she was wit it, so I took off her shirt. Man, her body was bangin. I felt her heart trembling; she was ready. From nowhere, she tells a nigga ta stop. At this point, we're half way there so you know I had to finish the job," Eric said with a grin. Marcus responded with curiosity, "even though she couldn't go through with it. That's foul." Eric's mood instantly changing, he frowned and said, "naw, you foul. Man she ain't thought about you once and you all up in my grill questioning me about her." Marcus began telling him how only punks force themselves on girls. There was a pause. Eric glaring at Marcus said, "blood, I'm telling you now, get out of my face and don't ever disrespect me again, or I'll show you how much of a punk I am." Marcus responded, "I'm not calling you a punk. I'm calling your actions punkish." Eric opened his hand and smacked Marcus. Marcus said he acted like he was retiring to go home, turned his back, and then punched Eric as hard as he could. The crowd gathered around yelling "it's a fight, it's a fight!" Marcus said he got two good licks on Eric, but Eric overwhelmed him with his size; he slammed him to the ground and started kicking him.

Eric found a hockey stick lying around and threatened Marcus with it, saying, "you lucky we cool, 'cause I should straight up bust yo head wide open." Eric walked away and some of the center's employees ran over to see if Marcus was okay. Marcus wondered where they had been when he was getting bombs dropped on him.

After Marcus finished his story, he turned away and I

playfully pushed him on the bed. "If you're so big and bad, fight me," I whispered in his ear. At this point, it was confirmed how much this kid liked me and how strong and influential my beauty was. Marcus's eyes buckled open in surprise and he jokingly said, "girl don't play with me like that." We wrestled, joked, and laughed all through the night. Grams decided it was time to go home and I must say I wasn't ready to go. I was honestly having too much fun. "Marcus, I guess I'll see you later."

Where Are You?

It was the weekend and I had just had a rough week. Finals had come and gone and this was the same week that our church had a revival. Some well renowned speaker from Trinidad was the guest speaker. Every day from Monday to Friday we had church and we got out very late, and I'm talking late. So when Saturday rolled around, my excitement level was irrepressible. I was ready to get into some trouble. A loud noised vibrated my room. It was Grams pounding on my door demanding to get in. I thought I had done something wrong again, but she entered with a great big smile, "guess what I have for you? It's your first forwarded letter, open it so we can see what it is." I was nervous about opening the letter. I thought it was my report card. This year had been a struggle and I wasn't the ideal student. I slowly opened up the envelope to find a handwritten letter. Relief wasn't the word, especially with Grams all over my shoulder. It wasn't a report card. The first line read:

> **Don't be shocked. Please take every word I write for the truth. Baby it's me, your mom.**

"Well what does it say girl?" Grams asked. "It's my momma. Grams, she's alive," I exuberantly screamed. It was summer, but I swear it felt like Christmas day. My mother was writing me after all this time, my prayers were finally answered. My grandmother's expression changed from a look of anticipation to a sigh of relief. "My baby is safe, praise the Lord! Shey continue to read, but read it aloud so I can hear," Grams joyfully requested.

> **I know you've been worried, but I'm okay. Momma has thought about you everyday, since I left. Terry thought it would be easy for the police to track us down had we kept in touch with you guys. We've been living off some money Terry says he had stored away, so life hasn't been rough as far as money is concerned, but running place to place has been stressful. I'll continue to write sporadically, whenever I get a chance, but I have to sneak to send every letter off. Terry would kill me if he found out I made contact with anyone at home. I am so ready to come home. Your face, your smile, your voice are always in my dreams. Please don't think for a second that momma doesn't love you. Tell your grandma that I love her very much also.**
>
> **P.S. I called last week, just to see if momma's phone number was the same. It was good to know it was; when I get a chance, I'll call you. I promise.**
>
> **Love Always,**
> **Momma!**

Retraced

After I completed reading my mother's letter, Grams kissed me on the head. Walking out the room, she turned around, paused and said, "See Shey, I told you the Lord answers prayers." Grams was so happy, but I became analytical, realizing what my mother was and wasn't saying. The fact that it took so long for her to contact her only child tells me that there was great danger in contacting us; more than she was eluding to. I could imagine how Terry was beating her, threatening her, just torturing my beloved mother. He had one thing right, if I knew where they were, I surely would've turned his butt in. I decided to call my boy Marcus. I felt a different connection the previous day, not romantically, but closer than before. Before I could pick up the phone, the phone rang.

"Hello," I answered. "Hey Shey, it's me, Marcus." "Marcus, I was just about to call to tell you something." Marcus excitedly said, "whaaat, that's a shocker. You call me. Well listen, I called to tell you something to." Hearing the vivacity in his voice immediately prepared me to want to hear his news first. "What is it Marcus?"

"Shey, you go first." "Remember a while back I told you about my mother," I said. He answered, "Yeah." My mother wrote me and she's alright. I'm worried about her, but at least I know she's alive," I told him. "That's good news. I wished I had some." Marcus continued, "My grandmother has been trippin'. She's been crazy worried about me, ever since that fight I had wit' yo boy. See, a coach from this high school in Flint wants me to play for his Catholic school on a full scholarship. The school starts from the 8th through the 12th grade. My grandmother thinks this is a great opportunity, plus they rank very high academically in the nation."

"Why so far, and how can you play varsity basketball as an eighth grader?" I asked. "I'll play junior varsity and have a chance to play on the varsity team when I hit the ninth grade," he answered. For 10 seconds there wasn't a response.

Retraced

I removed the phone and cleared my ears because I knew I misheard what he'd said. "Can you repeat that for me again?" My first thought was intertwined with the fact that someone I started to care about was leaving me. I mean Marcus was the little brotha I never had. Plus his words were uplifting. It was the very thing that helped our friendship grow. Words allowed me to feel a person's heart. And his heart was unlike any others. It's not like circumstances hadn't taken anyone else away from me. I should have been used to people leaving me. Bye Marcus.

Hood, I'm out!
MARCUS......

❧

Summer was coming to an end and it was the day for me to move to Flint. From the last conversation with Sheyla to now, it's been three weeks. Between those weeks of not talking to Shey, me and grandma have been setting up arrangements for my transition to Flint. I was moving in to stay with Coach Hutchskins. We had been in contact the entire summer; my grandmother and I also visited their home. Coach Hutchskins had been coming to my games on the weekends. He sent letters and kept in communication with my grandmother. I wasn't aware they had discussed the possibility of me playing in Flint, but I guess getting me safely out of Detroit had always been in the back of Grandma's mind. Coach H', as I respectfully called him, continued telling me how excited he was to have me join his team and his home. When I visited for the first time, his family seemed pretty nice. He had a son who played basketball for a division two college, another son named Lyle who was two years my senior, and two twin daughters, Jessy and Tessy, who were six. I didn't get a chance to meet the eldest son, but the one that was two years older than me was either competitive or had a point to prove to his dad. Within the first hour of meeting him, he challenged me in everything you can think of: one-on-one, video games, handshakes, I mean this dude had issues. My goal was only to fit in and make everyone feel comfortable having a black kid from Detroit come to live with them. Lyle was a kid that if we were in Detroit, I would've took him outside to the nearest court and humiliated him, straight put it on him, but I was sure I'd get my chance. I declined on every attempt he made. Coach H' realizing what his son was doing, abruptly pulled me aside into his home office and started talking to me about my basketball future with his school. "Stun, you'll have a chance to start varsity at the point guard position after your eighth grade year. I can't promise you a start, but I will give you the opportunity. Our starting point guard graduated and will enter his first year at the University of Michigan," he said. "Hooping," I suggested.

"Yeah, well not this year. He'll get red-shirted and have the chance to play the following year," Coach H' responding with pride. I felt pretty good at this point, because his program was getting players scholarships.

My goal was to go to a big name college where I could play on television in front of millions. As the day progressed, I became more comfortable with staying with the Hutchskins.

The big day was here, the time has come and I'm sad because I'm leaving my hood, my peeps. I had to call Dannie and Sheyla before I jetted. Dannie unexpectedly was very supportive. He said, "dawg, you got to get out of the 'hood, it's taking people under. With your basketball skills, you can go to the league (NBA.) and do some good for bruhs in the 'hood. Besides, think of all the honies that'll be riding your coattail. Stun can I get an autograph? Can I have your kids? Stun, can you let me drink your bath water?" Laughing, I immediately hung up with Dannie and called

Sheyla to say my last goodbye. Unfortunately, Shey wasn't around. Trying to reach her was a task and a half; without an answering machine, it's been impossible to say good-bye to her. "Grandma, before you take me to the Greyhound, can you take me over Shey's house," I asked. We went and again no Sheyla, so I wrote down my new address and slid it under their door.

Losing Basketball!

HOLY ROSARY, SENIOR HIGH SCHOOL FOR THE GIFTED. My first day was kind of weird because I was just this frail eighth grader mixed in with junior and senior high school students. I had never heard of a high school that had an eighth grade class. I guess they felt the school was Catholic, so the younger students didn't have to worry about being bullied. Coming from Detroit, that was the least of my worries, but being one of ten black students in the school made me feel awkward. After attending some of my classes, I knew I was in trouble.

"Class, for extra credit, we've been studying global warming. Based on our study of past climates, what does the relationship between changes in atmospheric CO_2 levels and changes in global temperature show? And please answer without looking at your notes." I slid in my seat trying to hide from having the teacher call on me. My eyes wandered around the entire room while every student sat up listening attentively as if they all knew the answer. At least 16 of the 22 students raised their hands with enthusiasm. "Well, lets pick someone whose hand wasn't raised," Mrs. Stew said. Boom, Boom-Boom, Boom, my heart pounded. I swore everyone could hear the sound bursting through my chest. The sweat glands were actin' a fool. I felt every drip of sweat leave my forehead landing on my desk. "Oh God, please don't let her call me," I mumbled under my breath. Her finger pointed toward me. "Yes over there."

"Mrs. Stewenski, it simply shows that changes in global temperature doesn't assure the same change will happen in atmospheric CO_2 levels," Simon, the student sitting right next to me answered. I looked at him in amazement. "Wooee, and this was only the eighth grade," I thought.

When gym class came around, I was relieved, anything to get away from those boring classes. The strong smell of sweat and chlorine from the nearby pool mixed in with the wax used for the gym floor put me in a state of familiarity, the place where I felt most comfortable; the schools basketball court. I stood back to watch these white cats play a pick up game of B-ball. There were other classes in the gym; 8th, 9th, and 10th grades. Some were pretty good and the few black kids were okay. I asked if I could get in a game and they looked at me like I was some skinny young punk with no skills. They sarcastically said yes. I smirked, thinking how I was about to show them how hoopers in Detroit play the game. After my team won three games straight, it seemed as if the entire gym watched me take advantage of everyone that checked me. After my show, we heard a whistle blow. Coach Hutchskins came walking in. He pulled me and three of the players I was playing with to the side. "Hey fellas, looks like you got an early introduction to your future teammate. Everyone started introducing themselves. By the time school ended, I had students going out of their way to introduce themselves to me, calling me the savior. Man, I was beginning to like my new horizons.

One month later, I decided to call Sheyla to see how she was doing. "Sheyla speaking," she answered. Feeling nervous as if it was my first time speaking with her I said,

"Hey girl it's your husband." "Heeey Treach, just kidding, what's up Marcus?" refusing to call me Stun, she giggled. It was truly refreshing to hear her voice again. She wanted to know how everything was going and I let her know that it was okay, everything besides the fact that Coach's son is a little jealous of all the attention I was receiving from the students and from his dad. During our conversation I noticed she wasn't being to respondent to what I was saying. Confused and frustrated I asked, "Shey, what's wrong? What's poppin' off in your head?"

"Nothin'," defensively she answered. As the conversation continued, she started to brag about this new boy she met, some knucklehead thug again. The same story brought about pre-explored frustrations for me. My ear became the funnel for her stories of love; my heart, a doormat for her developing licentious ways. Like a flash of lightning, it finally clicked in my head, maybe this was a battle I couldn't win. I could never fit her perception of an ideal mate, so it was important for me to get out of my fantasy world. Besides, I was a star athlete and I was much too young to be that caught up in some girl. If anything, she should be chasin' me around. This was my way of overcoming my frustration; just too bad I didn't really feel that way.

Weeks went by and not once had I picked up the phone to call Shey. It was also apparent that she didn't care to hear from me because not once had she tried reaching a brotha. I knew had she broken up with the dessert of the month she would've called me back, but I ain't no punching bag for anybody.

After reminiscing about Shey, Mrs. H' knocked on the door to tell me dinner was ready. No one could touch my Grandmother's cooking, but Mrs. H' was doing her thang. She even made good ole' soul food the way a black southerner would hook it up. On this day she made collard greens, fried chicken, corn and another side dish called perogies.

They begged me to try it, but I wasn't in the mood to try anything that had a name that sound like food for aliens.

Sitting at the dinner table, I asked Lyle if he was enjoying his sophomore year. "It's pretty cool, especially being I'm the starting point guard on the team," egotistically he voiced. I knew it was a shot at me to let me know that he had the position and was trying to rub it in my face. The first game of the season was in another two months. I was playing junior varsity. The anticipation wasn't as great for me because I could easily start on the varsity team. J.V. was going to be easy sailing. My biggest challenge was getting Lyle to put down his defensive guards and become friends with him. For God's sake, we were going to be living in the same house together for at least another two years.

One day Lyle was shooting jump shots in the gym. Looking at him I was able to see why his shot wasn't as consistent as it could have been. "Hey Lyle, you should try to find a comfortable form and practice shooting that same way no matter how many times you miss. Consistency in form will make you a better shooter, especially when your mechanics are on point." Lyle gave me a deep stare and instead of the response I expected, he said, "Thanks, but no thanks, I've been playing a little longer than you." He walked away and sent me off nodding my head in disbelief. I mean what had I done. His attitude made it a little uncomfortable in the Hutchskins household. I hadn't told Coach, but after three months of the tension, it was time to tell him. "Coach, for some reason Lyle doesn't like me and he's been pretty nasty towards me." After saying that, I noticed the twang in my accent was becoming a little more white surburbanish. I inwardly laughed at myself awaiting Coach's response. "Son, boys will be boys. Besides a little manly competition never hurt anyone." Okay, if coach wanted me to be more competitive with his son, I was going to punish him every time I took the court.

It was two weeks before the varsity and junior varsity season was to start. Coach set up a scrimmage between the varsity and the junior varsity teams. Bingo, my time to shine and to embarrass little Lyle. The whistle blew and it was on. Right off the bat, Lyle purposely elbowed me in the mouth. Then he tripped me when I was coming off a pick. Everytime I touched the ball he took out some sort of sneak aggression. Coach was acting like he hadn't seen anything. Physical play is a part of the street mentality, so I was use to playing physical basketball, but this was different. My man was straight up trying to hurt me. He continued and I just lost my cool. Swwooooop, the ball hit Lyle in the back after he turned away. "Punk, why did you throw the ball at me," Lyle yelled. "Punk, who you calling a punk," I immediately lashed out at him. I guess the hood was coming out of me at this point. As I charged at Lyle, one of the assistant coaches grabbed and dragged me out of the gym. Heading towards the locker room, I could see Lyle smirking and grinning.

The assistant coach was talking to me, but I blanked out. My mind was back in Detroit. Questioning how did I end up in this school. Basketball usually kept me out of trouble, but this time it got me caught up. Huffing and puffing, tears running down my face and no one to talk to. "Marcus, did you understand?" Coach Bradley asked concluding his talk. Knowing I hadn't heard anything but his question, I still responded with a "Yeah, Coach." As soon as I looked up, the locker room doors flung open. Coach H' storms in to confront me.

"What was that out there, Stun. How in the hell do you think you can bring that gangster Detroit basketball in my gym! We do not play like that! You have to learn how to control your temper. What if we were in a championship game and you did something like that. That is ridiculous! I am so disappointed in you. I'll have to suspend you for your first two games and you won't start for some games following your suspension."

"Coach, let me explain," I requested.

"No explanations needed. Now get in the shower and come back and watch practice from the bleachers!" Coach screamed.

My head was pounding. Pain took over my entire body. On a scale of 1 to 10, this migraine was a 10. This was the first time I'd had a headache in months. Putting myself in this mess of a living situation wasn't worth it. I couldn't wait to get home and call my grandmother. Lyle had know idea on how much I wanted to finish what we'd started. Rage consumed me and I needed to come back to Detroit. On the ride home, Lyle and I refused to talk or look in each other's direction. During the ride I got stuck on Coach H's words. Gangsta. Detroit. What did any of that have to do with what had just occurred? No one said anything to Lyle. I felt stereotyped, misunderstood and out of place. I knew I lost my temper, but man they acted as if Lyle hadn't played a part in this whole debacle. The more I thought about it, the more furious I became.

"Hey boys. Hi honey. Dinner's ready," Mrs. H' greeted us. I spoke, then rushed to my room to use the phone. "Grandma get me out of this place. I need to come home."

"Come home! Boy what happened?" Grandma asked. "I don't fit in. Lyle hates me, so he does things to get to me and coach lets him get away wit it. School is foul. White this and White that. Nothing about my peeps, as if Black people didn't play a part in history. No one talks like me. The only people who do come around are the young basketball groupies. Today I almost got in a fight with Lyle and when the coaches broke us up, no one listened or tried to understand my side. I was kicked out of practice. I'm just suffocating, help me please. Get me out of here," I pleaded.

"Hold on boy. You're rambling off at the mouth and actin' like you're not strong. All the mess you been through, you mean to tell me you went to Flint and got weak. Look, one of my girlfriends from the church talked to her sista that stays down there, call her. Her work number is 1 810-CITYKID. She does a lot with inna city kids; maybe she'll help you meet some friends. Granny has to go, I love you, be strong and take care!"

Talking to my Grandma helped me to focus on my goals, getting a good education and preparing for a good college. I looked at the number she gave me and called Ms. Priscilla. Turned out, Ms. Priscilla worked at the Boys and Girls Club on the northside of Flint. She asked to speak with Coach to get approval to pick me up this weekend. The northside resembled the eastside of Detroit, corner stores with all types of liquor, none owned by blacks, cars driving past with wannabe thugs bouncing their heads to the beat of the baseline from stereo systems pounding mufflers to the street. I felt at home. I went inside and played video games, met some homies and felt rejuvenated to talk to some real people. I didn't want to leave, but I knew I had to go back and deal with the H' family like a man.

After the first few games of my suspension were served, I thought I would get in to play. Our junior varsity team was 0 in 2 and I wasn't surprised 'cause they didn't have me on the floor. The next few games went by with our team losing and me not getting off the bench. The students that once called me the savior were now ignoring me like I had slapped their momma's or something. No Grandma, no Sheyla, no friends and now no basketball. My grades began to slip and my headaches became more frequent. Stress lived and I didn't.

I called my boy. "Dannie, what's up?"

"Who dis?" Dannie answered.

"It's Stun fool."

"So how is it living in the burbs?"

"Dannie man, I hate it. The girls are all stuck up. Our basketball team is terrible, I'm just ready to come back to the D." Listening to his stories, and how life was treating him in Detroit, it made me miss the hood.

Later in the week I asked Coach H' if I could speak to him in private. It was time for me to find out my role as an athlete and to let him know I wanted out. As he sat in his leather office chair, I noticed the stare he gave me. It was stern and uninviting. "What is it son? How can I help you?" I looked directly at him, swallowed and took a deep breath. " Coach, I know I was wrong for the blow up with Lyle, but I felt like I was treated unfairly." I took another swallow, realizing what I really wanted to say wasn't coming out and a more filtered down version was. "I'm down here to play basketball, and you're not letting me."

"Not letting you," he responded

"Coach let me finish. See, I know Lyle doesn't like me, he's your son and you're not feeling anything I have to say. I'm just not cool with this set up and I'm ready to go back to Detroit."

After listening to what I had to say, he sat up in his chair, took another big puff from his cigar. "Marcus, son, I'm teaching you discipline. I know Lyle is partly to blame for some things, but you have to find other ways to deal with your problems. In regards to basketball, it'll work itself out. You have all the ability in the world, eventually your time will come. The junior varsity season is almost over. I'm having a team play against the Detroit teams this summer for their summer leagues. You can play a part and continue to harness your skills for a chance to play varsity next year." This dude is in my face talking about *potentially* playing varsity. He sat up there and told me and my grandmother that varsity wasn't a problem, that I'll have a chance to start on varsity, but now he's saying *potentially* play on varsity, as if I might still be playing J.V. next year.

"Coach, you recruited me by telling me and my grand-mother I had a chance to start; now I feel like you lied to

Retraced

me," I said.

"Remember, you must earn your spot, nothing is given here," he said abruptly getting out of his chair telling me he had some urgent things to attend to.

Sitting there in a daze, licking my lips, I was on a straight up mission to wreck shop. Three games left in the season and I was ready. In practice I played perfectly, no show boating, just playing typical suburban basketball. Game time came, the junior varsity coach put me in the game. Forget that weak way of playing, I started breaking players ankles, straight putting it on this team. They were at my mercy. We ended the game winning by 15 points. I scored 30 points and had 18 assists. My first game and I broke the all time J.V. assist record. Of course the next three games we won and I averaged 22 points and 15 assists.

Just as I expected, school was different again. Teachers and students got a basketball buzz and were anticipating what would come next. Next year, next year is what everyone talked about. It's like a resurgence of the savior. It was sickening. Where were they when coach wouldn't let me play? Coach was so excited about what I had done. He was just as excited about the upcoming four years as everyone else was. Me, I was on some ole' Detroit vibe. I was trying to find a reason for me to go back to Detroit with my Grandmother's approval.

I called Ms. Priscilla from the Boys and Girls Club often, because I hated being in the Hutchskins house and she kept it real with me. She was very encouraging. She knew about the basketball hype, but didn't dwell on it. Ms. Priscilla would often tell me I would make someone a good husband. One conversation dealt with women liking attention and how they wanted to be spoiled by a man who was strong, sweet, but never a push over. It was a conversation that I sparked up a lot. With all her good and bad experiences, I felt like I was talking to Oprah Winfrey. Sheyla immediately came to mind.

"Ms. Priscilla, it's this girl back home that I really like, but I'm not her type, she's not feelin' me."

"Not her type, not feeling you. Boy, you are every girl's type handsome, smart, and going to be a star ball player. Any girl would be lucky to have you, just make sure she's not a bucket head; them kinda girls ain't nothin' but trouble." Spending time with her did me some good. Her tutelage filled my craving for motherly talk. When she spoke, I listened. Was Shey a hood rat? I didn't know and it really didn't matter, she was fly.

Summer Play

Throughout the year, my Grandmother said a Detroit high school coach continued to bug her about me. He said he had started this summer league basketball team comprised of some of the top talent in Detroit. He extended me an opportunity to play. Grandma left the decision up to me. It didn't matter who the coach was or who played on the team, I just wanted out of Flint, so it was no doubt that my answer was "when do I start?"

One weekend I took the Greyhound bus to meet my Grandmother and Coach Thomas. Coach Thomas was the coach of the RoadRunners and head basketball coach for The Murray Wright Pilots, a local high school team. I met two of the players for the RoadRunners, immediately knowing my decision was a great one. The RoadRunners traveled all over the country to play, giving players a chance to be seen by top college coaches. When he gave me the schedule, I noticed we were playing my high school coach's team. Man, I couldn't wait to get back to Flint to let Coach H' know I was playing for another team this summer.

The bus ride on the way back to Flint was full of anticipation. I wanted the Hutchskins to feel stupid, just to give

Retraced

the news to Coach and frog nose Lyle was heightening my thirst for revenge. I felt like they were using my name and reputation to attract attention from colleges to get Lyle looked at by some big named schools. My accusations were deep and out there, but I had to make some sense of why I was treated the way I was. Not being braggadocios, but I was probably the best talent that school had ever seen and they were playing me like a trumpet.

Pulling up to the Greyhound bus station, I saw Coach H' waiting in his Explorer truck. "What's up Coach," I enthusiastically spoke. "Hey, Marcus. How was the trip?" I just waited until the best time presented itself to tell him the updates.

"So buddy, are you getting set for the summer? We start practice right after you guys take your final exams. Lyle will be starting, but you'll be the sixth man off the bench, clocking a lot of minutes," Coach joyously uttered.

Talking about opportunities and time presenting itself perfectly. "Coach, I've decided to spend the summer in Detroit and play for a coach down there," I said with a straight face, trying to hold back my big grin. I just looked at him to see his reaction. He angrily looked in my direction. "What are you talking about? This is our way to prepare for the upcoming season." He massaged his hands through his hair, turned up his music and drove home without saying a word to me. I sort of nodded my head feeling accomplished.

Our varsity team didn't make the playoffs and our junior varsity finished the season with five wins and 6 losses. Classes had come to an end and I was packing up to go home to the 'D'. " I guess I'll see you on the 27th of July when we play y'all Lyle."

"I guess so Stun," he replied. Coach came in the room to see if I was ready to go to the Greyhound bus station. "Well Stun, make sure you stay healthy and come ready to play next year," Coach oozed out of his soul. He was gauging to see if I was making a permanent move. "Coach I'll see you in August and you know I'll be ready to play next year."

Entering Detroit reintroduced my smile to my face. I hadn't been that excited since the last time I hung out with Sheyla. "Hi, Mrs. Patron, may I speak to Shey."

"Hey Marcus, it's good to hear from you. Shey's not in right now, she's in Atlanta visiting some relatives for the summer, but I'll let her know you called."

Yeah I called as soon as I got to the crib. I wasn't sweating her, I just wanted to let her know I was back in town. After I left her a message, I called my boy Dannie. "What's up son? How you livin?"

"Stun, this you, What's up boy? I heard you're playing for Murray Wright's coach this summer."

"Yeah. He seems to be a cool guy to play for," I answered.

"Well you know that's the high school I'm going to." Dannie went on to say he was excited, because he was going to play junior varsity basketball.

"Why aren't you playing for him this summer," I asked. Dannie laughing and barely getting his words out, "man, you think I wouldn't if I could. You know he only got the stars playing. I guess I'm not a big enough name to play."

With my basketball schedule, it was impossible for Dannie and I to hang out. We talked on the telephone a lot. He was always interested in who I played with, who I met and if there were any honies hanging around. Hooping against some of the top high school players and meeting college coaches was cool, but hanging with Coach Thomas was better. He was big on teaching us the philosophy of basketball and becoming better mental players, not just relying on physical gifts. His wisdom and knowledge was impressive. Anytime I had questions bothering me, I would ask Coach Thomas. One day we were talking about God and he was explaining how Jesus Christ changed his life. Jesus was often a big part of his conversation and cleared some things up for me.

"Coach, why does God allow all this evil stuff to happen to people?"

"Son, God is the comforter that helps you through your struggles and builds character through your pain. He's not the source of your pain. Sometimes satan is, and a lot of times people are their own worst enemy. That's why I won't allow excuses on my basketball court. When you can overcome yourself, the sky is the limit," Coach responded. Between the balance of Ms. Priscilla in Flint and Coach Thomas, I almost had a balance of parenting. His words were principles for me to build on and to use to overcome my own personal struggles.

Playing with the best players in the state of Michigan didn't leave a lot of playing time for me, but the experience made me a better player and person. The summer games were coming to an end and it was time for us to play Coach Hutchskins and his son Lyle's summer team. Coach Thomas knew the situation and allowed me to start. I had so much fun playing and killing Coach Hutchskin's team. We beat them by 40 points. Coach H's son Lyle had 6 points. After the game, Coach Hutchskins gave me a hug and said, "save some of that for the season, I'll see you soon in Flint."

The summer had come and gone and I wasn't ready to return to Flint. The time I spent with Coach Thomas made me want to stay home even more. Just imagining playing for a coach who really cared made me resent Coach H.

My grandmother refused to let me come back home, no matter how many times I begged. After two successful basketball seasons on varsity playing for Coach Hutchskins, my sophomore year was coming to an end. I decided to meet the Athletic Director to let him know how unfair I was being treated. With me averaging 18 points the past two years, it was crazy to think I wasn't starting. Many of the college coaches that once pursued me dropped off. Our seasons could have been more productive, but our offense was centered around trying to make Lyle a star. It wasn't happening and it hurt scholarship opportunities for me and the other players.

Dr. Blue's door was cracked and I heard Coach's voice. I listened in to see if it was an appropriate time for me to disrupt their conversation. "Sir, Marcus isn't a team player and I'm thinking of kicking him off the team."

"Are you kidding me?" Dr. Blue questioned him.

" Sir, he's been very selfish and with him on the team next year. It'll hurt the team's chemistry, especially with Lyle going to college. Lyle's leadership won't be there to keep the team together," Coach Hutchskin answered.

"We brought Marcus here to bring recognition to the school, to give us a chance of winning. He's delivered on every level! You can't honestly believe your son received a basketball scholarship on his own pure ability. Marcus's name alone brought college scouts here and now that it has worked out for Lyle, you want to kick Marcus out. That is the most selfish thing I've heard coming from a colleague. You do not have my permission to do so. Get your act together and continue to win or it'll be you that we'll let go!" Dr. Blue said in a screeching controlled voice, trying not to allow others in on his anger.

Prostituted. That's exactly how I felt. No one had my best interest at heart and me and my grandmother were deceived, tricked. There was no way I was going to continue to play for this school. Fearing my grandmother wouldn't believe me, I decided to skip the rest of my classes and called Ms. Priscilla from an outside pay phone. Without question, she believed every word I told her. She told me to go back in the school and she would meet me at the end of the day.

Throughout the day, I did whatever I could to avoid

Coach and his son. In fact, every person I looked at reminded me of all the lies. It was impossible for me to believe that everyone was involved in this mockery, but it sure felt like it. Everyone was an enemy and I was leaving this city and this school whether my Grandmother allowed me or not.

Right before my last class let out, Ms. Priscilla was already entering the building. I marched right down to the main office to meet her. After she received a visitor's pass we went straight to Dr. Blue's office.

Dr. Blue greeted us at the door. "Hey Marcus, how is everything going. How may I assist you?"

"Apparently Marcus was asked to attend this school under false pretenses," Ms. Priscilla interrupted.

"Mam, before I reply to this ridiculous accusation, who are you?"

"Sir, this is my mother," I answered. Amusingly shocked, Ms. Priscilla sort of looked in my direction and smiled in admiration. "Marcus, I was under the impression that your mom was deceased," Dr. Blue said. Ms. Priscilla interrupted again. "Let's deal with the matter at hand. Marcus says you guys may kick him off the team and that he was only brought hear to bring notoriety to a school that hadn't been respected athletically in ten years. Is this true?"

The room came to a complete silence with Dr. Blue in a fight to find the words to respond. "Well, yes and no, don't, don't take it out of proportion." I stared in his eyes and he knew I really knew the truth. "Look, son. Okay, maybe you're right, but please believe I really did want the best for you and the best for our school. I personally felt you could give our school a chance to win and in return we'd give you an outstanding education. Forgive me."

My anger wasn't directed towards Dr. Blue, I believed him, but it was Coach Hutchskins who did all the lying and only him that deliberately made my life a living hell.

"Sir, I have to leave. This is not what I came to this school for; my basketball career is being sacrificed here."

"Young man, I understand. Make your grandmother proud and do what is in your best interest," Dr. Blue whispered with a tear in his eye. Coach H' was suspended with pay for the remaining months of the school year.

Afterwards, Ms. Priscilla said I could stay with her to finish out my last three months at Holy Rosary Senior High School For the Gifted. We went over to the Hutchskins house and I left them a note with the key to their house attached letting them know they wouldn't be hearing from me again. After packing all of my belongings, we called my grandmother on the three-way. She heard the disappointment in my voice, respected Ms. Priscilla's advise, and decided to allow me to come back home to Detroit.

I immediately contacted Murray Wright's coach, Coach Thomas, letting him know what happened and that I was hoping to come play for his team. Our conversation lasted for an hour. The excitement in his voice confirmed that home was the place for me.

No Line Between Love and Pain
SHEYLA

Entering the house, looking at my Grandmother's eyes reminded me of how much I disappointed her. Tasha had become my security blanket and we did everything together. Our relationship was a thorn in my Grams side because she continued to feel my disobedience was a result of my developing friendship with Tash. Grams and I drifted so far apart; it was hard for her to understand me, considering everything I did to be purposely degenerate and malicious. I must admit, some things I did were strictly out of spite, but some were results of me protecting me. Tasha had proven herself to be down for me. Grams was too committed to the church to even see what it was I was dealing with.

Even my boy Marcus bussed up. Just when I felt like he was going to be there for a sista, he left, just like my mom. What about a father? It would be easier to accept my dad being killed in the streets or was just ignoring me like most fathers, the fact is, my dad, oh, he's just a rapist. This cat had to have been a sick pervert to rape a lady and deposit part of him in her. How crazy is it knowing that I'll never know my dad, and if I did, would probably try to kill that nigga. I was a rejected soul. I ain't have nothin', so when Tash and I were introduced to dudes that had game, money, and respect, it made me feel like somethin'. Most dudes were always on a front, acting like they had loot. When a guy couldn't do nothin for me, he was out the door.

The summer that Marcus left was without major drama. My grandmother finally let up on some of her strict ways. She was advised to do so by someone she respected, her Pastor's wife. Apparently she had dealt with some of the same issues with her oldest daughter. Church had finally worked in my favor for once. The boys started calling my house and it was on from that point on. One day Grams walked up to my room, "Hey Shey, Mrs. Caroline said Marcus asked about you, and had been trying to reach you. Maybe you should return his phone call."

Out of sight, out of mind was how I felt when Marcus left. No need for me to deal with a friend that couldn't do anything for me. The summer went fast. I spent most of that summer in Atlanta working a summer job. The little money I saved, I spent on clothes. Everything had to be right for me to come in as a freshman and rule. High school was about to meet the Queen, Sheyla Patron.

Hey Shey,

We're moving again. It's getting pretty hot here. Terry feels like the police are catching up to him. He's become very paranoid, which makes him angrier. I'm writing because you should be entering high school now. This is a great part of your life. I want you to make sure you enjoy it. It's a small window that closes fast, so please think about the choices I made

and do the opposite. I voluntarily locked myself into a cell of dependency and fear without an escape. I'm out here staying strong and surviving, so don't worry 'bout me. We'll see each other I promise. All the pain I put you through, I guess I'm being punished now. Know this, I didn't reject you. Emotionally, I must admit that it was hard to deal with the fact that my love for you was so strong, yet I hated part of what you represented. I guess subconsciously it ate at me. Sometimes I pretended that the rape had never occurred. It allowed me to live in a fantasy and helped me to love you. You were the one that was truly the victim. Having Terry around helped me remain in the fantasy, as if he was your father. But the love he gave to you was nonexistent. I was too weak to come to grips with it. Being away from you made me realize that what the devil meant for evil, God can make good. You are the glue that continues to hold me together. I can't wait to see you. Please forgive your mother!

P.S. Shey, Tell my mother that I'm beginning to understand what she tried to teach me for years. This is an inside message, she'll understand.

Love Momma 4life!

The emotional drama queen I am, I started crying, recognizing her pain. The kind hidden under thick skin, invisible to the human eye, but recycled in daily life. The letter from her encouraged me; the hope of seeing her soon seemed to be a real possibility. That possibility later proved to be a lie.

For the first year of my high school career, I ran to get the mail whenever I heard the mail lady open our mailbox. Always nothing! My mother had disappeared again continuing the same cycle. The letter I held and carried with me everyday was thrown away in the wind, it was time for me to release my pain and frustration and just let it go.

In high school, I flirted a lot with boys, but maintained my virginity. The attention I got from young men substituted the true love I lost and didn't receive from my mother. Being a virgin never stopped boys from trying to holla and become my first intimate partner. One thing that kept me confident in who I was, was that no one could claim me as a slut. My reputation was unblemished, unlike some of my girls like Tasha.

One day after school, me, Tash and the girls were hanging in front of the school. Boom, Boom, Boom. The base from a nearby truck blasted in our chests and thumped in our ears making it hard for us to talk. After a while, the sounds went mute. Beep, Beep! A horn blowing, getting my attention. "Hey, baby, can you come here for a sec.?" A strange voice asked. I pointed to myself and he nodded yes. "Girl, whoever that is needs somebody's attention. He's in an OJ too," Tasha spoke out the side of her mouth while staring at the truck. Everyone remembers seeing OJ Simpson riding down the highway with his boy A.C. in a white Bronco truck after being accused of the murders of Ron Goldman and Nicole Simpson. We called Bronco's from that point on, OJ. This OJ was trimmed in candy apple red with highlighted red flakes covering the exterior paint. It sat on D's demanding attention, definitely catching mine. It really didn't matter who was driving. This man must have had some money. "You look familiar and I never forget a face," he said. Even though he looked familiar to me also, I just took it as a coincidence and a sorry pick up line.

"What's your name sexy?"

"Sheyla," giggling as I answered.
"Sheeeyla, Sheyla, Shey- la that name rings a bell."
"Well, what's your name?"
"My name is Ja'Ron."

I immediately zeroed in on who he was. His thick eyelashes looked in oddity, showcasing his glowing eyes. I acted like I didn't know who he was and let him continue to beat his mind up trying to figure out how we knew each other. His complexion was dark and he had a smile that could brighten up heaven. He stepped out of his truck and drew me in. My eyes marveled at his entire frame from his toes to his head. I bit my lip to hold back the scream that wanted to announce how fine he was.

"I give up," he said.
"Aren't you Eric Black's brother?"
"That's how I know you! You not little Sheyla no more huh!"
"I guess not. So how is Eric doing?"
"He's ayight. He got into something deep and is outta state on the run. He's never coming back here. You know whatam saying," Ja'Ron said in his mellow voice.

I wasn't going to be nosy and ask what he did, but knowing Eric and his temper he probably killed somebody. Kicking it with Ja'Ron made me forget my girls were waiting. Boys never made me nervous, but Ja'Ron was a man and he had me frazzled.

"Come on girl," Tasha called out from across the street.
"Here I come." Ja'Ron was always the finer of the two Black brothers and now he was trying to holla at a sista. Before I departed, he gave me a flier and invited me to a gig he and his boys were giving. "Shey, just give the doormen my name. Tell them who you are and that you're my guest. Don't worry about I.D. or the cover charge, I gotchu," winking as he gave the invite. I told him okay and that Tasha would be coming with me. Walking away, I noticed him

staring at my back side, so I swiftly swung my hips side to side giving my normal walk an extra umph.

"What was that all about," Tasha's curiosity bursting out of her grin.

"Girl, that was Ja'Ron Black."

"Whaaat, I heard he was getting em, but I didn't know like that. Plus I heard he's a little crazy." A lot of people knew Ja'Ron was doing pretty good in the dope game. I had been hearing his name drop around the hood for a minute, but I hadn't seen him since I was in junior high school. It was strange to feel for him the way I did. I mean, he brought about that same feeling I had when I first met his brother Eric. I couldn't wait to see him again.

Grams was doing her usual church thing, so when she left, Tasha picked me up in her boyfriend's car. My little mini body dress caressed my curves. My hair was whipped, so I knew Ja'Ron was about to be all on me. The night blew a slight wind, making my hair flow with each breeze. Surveying the competition from a distance, I noticed how much Tash and I stood out. Approaching the club, The Clue, I could see that we weren't the only girls vying for attention. All the girls had breasts, legs, thighs, hamhocks and anything else you could imagine exposed. My patience is short, so I couldn't wait in a long line, so I just went to the front and said "hey, my name is Sheyla and I'm a guest of Ja'Ron Black." The doorman looked at me and asked how many were with me. Tasha looked at me like I had presidential rank. "Ohkaay," she sang out.

I'm up in the club with people three to five years older than me. All the women that were in line came in staring at us with much hate; it felt good. To me their disgust represented power. We walked through the club. The sounds were cranking and the atmosphere was on fire. In the middle of the floor, girls were massaging the men private areas with their curvy roundness. Now that was dirty dancing. I asked

Tasha to come with me, but she couldn't resist the dance floor, it pulled her in like a magnet.

I began to survey the crowd looking and asking people had they seen the promoter of the party. After thinking to myself, I figured it being his party and all he was probably setting up to make a late grand entrance, so I went to join Tasha on the dance floor. Suddenly, from behind, I smelled this sweet fragrance of Fahrenheit cologne and a hand gently running down my bare arm. "I didn't think you were coming," The calm voice urged me to turn around. It was him, Ja'Ron.

"Hey. Well I'm here, so what's up?"

"Nothin', I'm just privileged to have you here," he said with a scintillating voice. We danced to two slow jams and just sat and kicked it. He was a smooth brother obviously experienced in dealing with women. Every word was with confidence and straight forward. He meant what he said and said what he meant. There was no question that I was dealing with a real man.

The night was coming to an end for me because I had to beat my Grams to the crib. "Thanks for the invite and the dance, but now I gotta get home," I whispered in his ear.

"Shey, I can't let you go without you taking this with you," pulling out a card with his pager number on it. He slipped it down my blouse, the part that exposed my cleavage. After rushing Tasha out of the party, I tried to play as if I wasn't all in. You know, acting like I was in control of this situation with an older man.

My girl Tash saw straight through me. "Girl, you let that boy get in yo' head didn't you?" There was no need to respond, I just looked at her as if to say no. My attention turned directly toward trying to beat my grandmother home. I had been avoiding friction with her as much as possible. The drama between she and I wasn't needed. I stepped in the house and hung up my jacket in the nearby closet.

Retraced

"Grams. Grams." Wooo, she wasn't home. My feet were aching so I threw my shoes to the corner, sat on the couch and propped my feet on the night stand. I just thought about the nice time I had.

After relaxing, I heard the keys at the front door. Grams came in cheery and asked how everything was going. While she and I talked, I turned on the T.V. and two familiar faces appeared. First, it was Eric Black. They said the 17 year old recently murdered a cashier during a botched burglary attempt and was on the run. No surprise, just like I thought. The second face was a mug shot of Terry Clemons. "Grams, hurry up come here!"

The news was reporting Michigan's Most Wanted-Past and Present. They talked about the murder of Calvin Littleton. As they described the events, it brought everything back to my remembrance. Reliving the events was mortifying. Man, my mom was with this chump.

> **Terry Clemons, also known as T.C., may be traveling with a companion by the name of Kim Patron. We think Terry may be connected to some unsolved robberies and other murders in the Metro area. If you see Terry Clemons, please alert the police and don't try to apprehend him yourself. He's considered armed and very dangerous.**
>
> **This is Rich Gatzer for Channel 7 News signing off!**

I immediately took a deep breath. Grams and I just stared at each other without saying a word. I knew then, mom was facing some major legal issues and I was scared for her.

Moments later…Ring, Ring. "Hey girl, I saw the news.

Retraced

I'm just calling to see if you're straight." It was Tasha. This was why I loved her so much, she had my back and really cared in her own way, even though she was the cause of most of my trouble with Grams.

After that night, Ja'Ron met me up at school everyday. Our friendship was growing. The more he came around, the more the high school girls resented me. The attention was marvelous. Ja'Ron had the tightest truck in the city and he was always geared. Fellas couldn't compete with him and girls didn't have the man that all dudes wanted to be. I was in heaven and loving it.

Clothes were no longer a desire. Ja'Ron kept me in fly gear. My Grams was concerned with my new found wardrobe, but there really was no need to explain. It wasn't her bizness, but like always I gave her an explanation.

"Sheyla, you better not be doing anything illegal out there."

"Grams, I'm not, everything is cool, trust me."

"Well you better not be doing anything for these young punks to give you all these clothes."

She might as well have called me a slut. She was always accusing me out of the blue.

"Grams, one of my girls' moms owns a small store and she gives clothes to her daughter and I to wear for advertisement in the school."

I couldn't believe my grandmother went for that. I think old age was finally catching up to her because she usually would've interrogated me to she found out what it was she was looking for. "Maybe God existed after all," I thought. He sure saved my butt.

Ja'Ron couldn't call me at my house, but I could call him. We would arrange a certain time for me to call him. It was nerve wrecking keeping things from Grams, but it was worth it, because; I was in love.

Ja'Ron had been hinting towards getting me in bed with

him. I knew I wasn't ready, but if anyone was going to be my first, it was going to be him. After a while, the pressure started captivating my thoughts. He started to mention sex everyday, so it was always on my mind.

"What's up bey, can I get that tonight?"

My heart said no, but my body needed it. What ate at me most was that he could get it from practically any girl he wanted and how else was I going to keep him in my life. I always dreamed of my first time being special. Waking up the next day in a big bed with rose petals falling from the ceiling. Three months into our relationship he asked with an aggression that spelled trouble. I could feel he was on the verge of sexing it up with some groupie chick around the way. "Okay, let's do it," I whispered in his ear. My fear was pregnancy. All the teens I knew with a kid struggled a lot. My heart craved for attention, and having a kid would take away from my wants, yet I knew to keep up with this lifestyle, I had to do my womanly duties. Ja'Ron urgent need to be with me didn't make it any better. He drove me to one of his boy's houses after school. "Dawg, I need to borrow your room for a sec, straight," he demanded of his boy, Tone.

"No problem, just clean yo mess up," Tone responded. Scared and nervous about my first time, I didn't take time out to think about how foul it was for Ja'Ron to take me over some dude's house to a bed that probably beds all of the boys in their crew.

My heart started beating so fast that I could feel the blood flushing through my veins. Ja'Ron stared me in the eyes and started to remove his clothes. He immediately brushed against me and started taking off my blouse and skirt. Out of my shyness, I turned around having my back face him to take off my under garments. He then grabbed me, and slowly turned me towards him. I hugged him as he laid me on the bed. His lips massaged every inch of my flesh as I began to quiver. Purring sounds reeked out of my mouth. As he entered, I screamed. The pain was unfamiliar and it wasn't feeling good at all. I bit my lip to hold back the words stop. I just wanted to please him.

We entangled in a grip of passion for 15 minutes. His sweat had the bed drenched. Ja'Ron immediately got up and told me to put my clothes on. I couldn't believe I'd experienced my first time and it wasn't anything like I thought it would be. My innocence was gone. My virginity wasn't my gift anymore. I gave it away.

Facing Grams was hard. I could no longer look her in the eyes. She was a wise lady. Letting her look me in the eyes would have revealed my secret. As I opened the door, there she was waiting.

"Hi, Grams."

"Hey baby, why are you so late? I thought you guys had a half day."

"Me, Tash and the girls hung out around the school for a few hours." Her eyes questioned my story. I started breathing hard, preparing myself for the verbal massacre.

"Okay, well I'm going to visit Mrs. Caroline's church to today, I'll be back later. Love you."

My held breath slowly gasped through my mouth. Man! She scared me straight. I was sure she could see my virginity missing from my soul. I ran so fast up the stairs to take a shower. I wanted to talk to someone, but who could I let know without condemnation. Even Tash would have been disappointed. I think she respected my innocence. My sexual encounter was weird, it wasn't romantic, it hurt, and I was sort of disappointed in myself.

My feelings carried over to the next day. In school I was pretty reserved and it was noticeable. Our crew sat in the middle of the lunchroom where we could see any and all the action; also it allowed us to be seen. Sitting at the table, Tasha began cracking jokes on all the broke dudes trying to holla at the girls at our table. Usually I participated, but this time I was in a daze. "Shey, what's up with you. You been quiet all day."

"Oh nothing, just chillin."

"Girl you know you can holla atcha girl, so what's really poppin in that head of yours?" Tash asked.

"I SAID NOTHIN!"

"Daaaaang!" All the girls sang in unison. Tasha looked like a flashbulb went off in her brain.

"Shey, I know you hung out with Mr. Black after school. So what happened?" Tash provokingly asked.

"Would y'all please quit digging for something that's not there!" I said with much attitude. After lunch was over, Tasha pulled me aside and asked had I lost my virginity. This girl knew me and could read me like a book. She suggested that I get over it, understanding it wasn't the end of the world. Talking to her helped me out. It removed the burden of me letting someone know the secret.

Two days went by and I hadn't heard from Ja'Ron. I called during my usual time, but no answer and he wouldn't return my page. I thought he was turned off by the other day, so rejection set in. The weekend had come and I wanted to spend time with him. Our relationship had gone to another level, I shared a part of me with him that no one else could claim, but him, so I called him again.

"Hey guy, whats been up?"

"Shey, hey girl, I was just thinking about you."

At once I was relieved. My heart was flaming with a connection that desired to see him.

"I can't tell. I haven't heard from you and I just wanted to see you," I responded.

"I could tell the other day was your first time and I wanted to give you time to yourself. I mean your virginity meant a lot to me. This was my way of respecting you."

Now what he said was full of game. I was too smart to

Retraced

fall for that wacked line, but I wanted to believe it with my heart, which blinded me into foolishness. A few hours later he met me a block away from my complex in the projects. We drove to his boy's house again, which was good with me. I wanted a second chance to show him how much of a woman I was.

He grabbed me by my hair and it was on. No pain this time. It was good and he made me feel like I was on another planet. Ecstasy and passion penetrated the air and then it happened, totally out of the blue. "I love you." The words were forced out by emotion, even though I tried to hold them back. "I love you, Ja'Ron," came out again. He continued doing his thing. No response, just ignoring my plea for affection. Inside I started to cry because I knew how precious this moment was to me and I knew there was no returning from where my feelings for him had gone. Infatuation consumed me.

INFATUATION

❧

The talk of the entire school was about some boy coming from Flint to join our basketball team. It was rumored that he was one of the best basketball players in the State. Our team wasn't terrible, but they couldn't make it pass the first game of the City playoffs. Our coach had never had a losing season. Coach Thomas had always gotten the most out of his players and this year wasn't any different. Our players weren't good enough to make it to the playoffs, but with good coaching, they did.

I wasn't a big supporter of sports. Everything involved was beneath me. The cheerleaders, the players, and the groupies were immature and uninteresting. Besides, the only thing I thought about was school ending and hanging out with my new boyfriend. After school, Tash called me. "Hey, Shey guess what?" Tasha blurted with excitement. Knowing Tasha, I was scared to guess. My girl was straight up wild. "What is it Tash?" She took a deep breath and proceeded to tell me how her cousin over heard Ja'Ron telling his boy that he bought an expensive chain for his girl. "Now Shey, let him be the one to reveal this to you. Girl, maybe Ja'Ron isn't a playa and is really diggin' you. Do yo thang and teach me some tricks while you're at it." The first thing that came to my mind was my man never was a playa in the first place, those were just rumors; second, I was excited and expecting a new chain.

As soon as I got off the phone with her, I got a head start on coming up with a fabrication to explain the chain to my Grams.

Weeks had gone by with me hearing from Ja'Ron only sporadically. And no mention of the chain. I explained it to myself as a misunderstanding or guessing he probably gave it to his mom. Oh well, I wasn't letting that rain on my party, so I thought. Tasha asked me everyday, "Shey did he mention the chain." I began to become more embarrassed over the situation.

I wondered what was up with him. He started to treat me like I was just some groupie girl jocking him for his money. Some people feared him, but I still saw the gentleness in him and I thought he was slowly changing. One day I decided to page him 911, over and over and over and over again. He finally responded. "What's up with you?" He impatiently asked. "Uh, we need to talk."

"Okay, talk then," he responded.

"Well, not over the phone, in person." As he finished his sentence, I heard a girl's voice in the background. "Who is that?" I asked.

"Man, I'll holla at you in a minute." Wham, he hung the phone up. Teardrops flowed and met underneath my chin.

Three hours later he called from a pay phone down the street. I went to meet him to see what was up with his recent behavior. "Hey, Ja'Ron, what's up with us?"

"Shey, you trippin. Just chill out please."

"Chill out, are you kidding? You've been treating me wrong and I know about the chain you bought, but who did you give it too? Some girl huh!"

Ja'Ron immediately grabbed my face and pushed me

back into the bushes. My mind immediately retraced back to the time I last saw T.C. flip out on my mother. I had become her and now understood the vulnerability of being infatuated.

"No one ever questions Ja,Ron," he responded in third person. "Anything I buy is for me and I don't have to report to anyone on where my money goes! Now get yourself together and get in the car." Without hesitation, I did exactly what he said. He apologized and we went to Red Lobster to eat. My conversation was forced. I really didn't have much to say because I was hurt. Not by the fact he became physically aggressive, but my mind was caught on the gold chain. Who did he give it to? How stupid, I totally ignored what had happened. I was more worried about if he was cheating on me.

After a month, I learned to never question him. He usually responded with gifts and attention. No matter what he did, I always excused it. "Is that a black eye I see," Tasha asked while gently touching my swollen eye.

"Yeah, it happened while me and Ja'Ron was play wrestling. He accidentally elbowed me in the eye"

"Yeah, he elbowed you alright. Now tell the truth and shame the devil."

"I told you what happened now leave it alone!" I said with a high pitch voice of defense.

"Well what did your grandma say?" Tasha asked.

"Not much. I told her someone threw a football in gym and it hit me in the face."

"Girl, you're starting to lie more than me. I can't believe your grandma is going for them," Tash rebutted. She stared at me in great disappointment. "If that fool ain't actin' right, you besta get that money and leave." How crazy was it to have her out of all people concerned with my situation, Ms. Wild thang herself.

OVER TASH CRIB

꽃

Hanging out at Tasha's house, smoke consumed the room and everyone was coughing up cloud puffs. The toxins from the marijuana leaves were flowing through the room as strong as ever. This was just another weekend with my girl Tasha. I had never smoked a blunt. Peer pressure had never gripped me into submission, but this day was different. Everyone was having fun, except me. My mind was caught on the wherabouts of a man who said he loved me with words, but whose actions often contradicted. "Hey, let me see that." Instantly the room got quiet and everyone turned to look at me. "Girl, don't play with the mari. If you going to hit it, then hit it, but if not, just chill," Tasha's cousin said in the midst of his coughing. "Y'all don't encourage my girl, she ain't into blazing," Tasha coming to my defense. "Tash, I'm straight, I got this," I said. I took the blunt and puffed twice. Everyone started coaching me. "Hold it in, Hold it in." I tried and instantly started coughing. They all busted into laughs. "Roookiiiie."

As the night progressed, inhaling became easier. I was blew out. "I can't let my girl go home like this. What are we going to do?" Tasha screamed. I started to giggle. Everything was hilarious. There was no controlling my laughter. Tasha went upstairs to get some smell good and sprayed me down with her mom's best cologne. She gave me some sunglasses and she and her boyfriend took me home. Luckily Grams was nowhere insight. One hour after entering the house, the phone rung. "Hello."

"What's up shawty, I'm about to come through." Thirty minutes later, a knock at the door. It was Ja'Ron. "Boy, what are you doing? You know my Grams would have my neck if she knew a man was here this late to visit me."

"Well, what do you want me to do, go home?"

"Naw. Come in quietly and go upstairs."

How stupid was I to take a chance like this? I had no idea where Grams was or when she was coming back. When I followed behind Ja'Ron upstairs to my room, I heard keys in the door. Keeping my composure was hard. I was still a little high from the get together over at Tash's house, but this little predicament immediately blew me back to some of my senses. "Hide in my closet," I whispered. Grams came up the stairs and said hi, then made her way to her bed. Ja'Ron stepped out of the closet and said, "This is turning me on." He began kissing me and squeezing me with his strong hands. He used his tongue to tickle my ears, which made me excited. "Sheila, I mean Sheyla, you smell like weed. You been smokin?" I didn't answer. I could swear this fool called me another name. The next thing you know I was making noises that spelled trouble. The excitement was out cold. I mean with the danger of Grams potentially walking in while I was embraced in delight was intensifying the moment. Being with him had a way of making me forget how mad I was supposed to be. After we did our thing, he wouldn't look me in my eyes. While putting on his clothes, I noticed scratches on his back. I knew they didn't come from me. Staying away from conflict and his violent ways, I didn't question it. As he snuck downstairs to leave, I immediately began to shed tears, just thinking about him sleeping with someone and then coming over to sleep with me. I couldn't sleep. The only thing that made me feel better was being optimistic, talking myself into believing there were other possibilities that could have lead to the scratches on his back.

ALL IS FORGIVEN

The more our relationship progressed, the more my life became entangled in the lifestyle of rolling with a baller. We ate at the finest restaurants and he bought me some very expensive clothes. My wardrobe had built up into a closet fit for a queen. Ja'Ron was invited to a release party of some up and coming rap artist from Detroit. Reluctantly Grams allowed me to spend the night with Tasha after constant begging. Tash's moms was like our friend.

She was down with letting me hang out all night. She even offered one of her baddest dresses that I was all set to wear until Mr. Ja'Ron pulled up. He rented a Benz Limousine. It was like a scene in the movies when he stepped out. He had this red Versace dress in one hand and flowers in the other. The dress fit like a glove, making me feel like a black Princess Diana. "Yes Dawling," screeched out of the side of my mouth. Entering the limo I noticed all the lights glowing from front to back. "You want anything to drink," Ja'Ron said while pointing to the bar next to us. I had never been in anything like this before, so I was reveling in how important I felt. The inside of this ride was plush, decked out in leather seats that adjusted to your body structure. I promise it felt like the darn thing was hugging me.

Everything about the night was perfect. We rubbed elbows with some big time politicians, local business owners and other prominent people in the metro area. We even met big hip-hop executives like Heavy D. Just hanging out with my boo set me up for failure when it came to dealing with guys my own age. How could anyone compete with this? Even when I caught Ja'Ron in lies and he became physically outraged, he always knew how to make it up to me. He placed me in high society, which defined what the Cinderella syndrome was all about. I became addicted to the big time and going back to regular old Shey, hanging with the high school homies was impossible to do, or so I thought.

At school, I over heard basketball players talking about how out cold they were going to be next year cause of this one player from Flint transferring to our school. The varsity players thought using basketball was the way to get a girl. I admit they had groupies, but when they stepped to me with that weak trash, it was a waste of breath. "Shey, you dropped something, can I pick it up," one guy asked. "What was it," I responded. "A conversation, so what are you doing Saturday?"

"Oh something that doesn't include you," I said. All of his fellow basketball players were like ooooh, dawg she got 'n' you. I even had to laugh, then walked off. "Hey girl AND WHERE HAVE YOU BEEN? I called you all weekend," Tasha meeting me face to face as I turned the corner in the hallway.

"Tash, you know I was with Ja'Ron."

"You better get more control over yo feelins. That boy will have you selling drugs for him in a minute. Can't nothin' good come out of messin' with a guy like him," Tasha unknowingly spoke prophetically.

"Thank you for your concern, but Sheyla Patron is the captain running this relationship. I thought you knew," I said, knowing there wasn't a piece of truth coming out of my mouth.

My sophomore year ended with me contemplating dropping out of school. I got nothing from it. The games, the child like behavior, the jealousy, everything bugged me about high school. Outside of Tasha, I really couldn't trust anyone. I was thinking about asking Ja to move in with him. If he had asked, I would have done it at the drop of a dime. Every material thing was easily possessed. There was nothing that I wanted that he wouldn't buy for me. Having nothing going to having everything was every girl's dream. I didn't need education to give me the goods in life. Ja'Ron was my escape. Going to school became a feat that challenged me.

My Grams wouldn't have allowed me living with some grown dude. She would've reported me to social services, and would have put Ja'Ron up under the jail had she known anything was up between us. Half the summer was sneaking around with Ja'Ron, the other half was trying to keep watch on Ja'Ron and his extracurricular activities. There was always an excuse for all the rumors about other women.

It was a few days before my sweet 16 birthday. Ja'Ron bought me this scandalous two carat diamond bracelet. I hid it from Grams because there was no way to explain this one to her. I was so excited. I couldn't wait to begin the school year with my jewelry. The haters really were going to be hatin'.

No Love at Second Sight

✻

Tash and I didn't really see a lot of each other during the summer. She was starting her career as a dancer, striptease that is. She was too young to dance at the bars, but that didn't stop her. She stripped at bachelor parties, after-hour-joints, basically anywhere they would allow her to dance without proof of age. Oh, my girl kept money. We walked in school and everybody identified true royalty. Dressed in Gucci, Versace, Guess, you name it, we had it and sporting my new bracelet, how could we be ignored? The fellas did any and everything to be in our presence except to bow. 2:10 came and it was time for me to go home. Walking the halls, someone came from behind and covered my eyes. "Guess who?"

"I ain't trying to guess, now get your fingers from over my eyes. I don't know where your hands been."

"Hey kidd, I ain't trying to get beat down. As he removed his hands, I turned and his smile met my eyes. "Marcus, is that you?" I asked with a surprise look on my face. "What up Shey, it's me, your husband," Marcus smiling with delight. He was tall and had put on a little weight. I had to admit, much better. One thing he really had going for him was his pretty teeth. "Wait a minute, you're not the basketball player that everyone was so excited about."

"I don't know. I guess that could be me."

"Well, welcome to Murray Wright."

"Thanks." He gave me a big hug. "I'll be seeing you around. Keep in touch," I said walking away. "Shey, you get finer the older you get," Marcus screamed down the hall. It was good seeing Marcus again. He was living his dream being known as this big basketball player and all.

Tash met me at the door as I was leaving out. "Guess who I saw today." "Let me guess, Michael Jackson," Tash said with a big grin on her face. "Oh, you got jokes. But naw, Marcus Stunson. He's the basketball player that everyone in school has been talking about."

"What, you mean the little puny guy that had a crush on you."

"Girl, he's not puny anymore," I said as Marcus was coming towards us.

"Hey, Tasha. You still look the same. Y'all still kickin it, huh. Well, I'll be seeing y'all. I got to go to the store to get some juice before basketball conditioning starts," Marcus blurted out as he rushed out the door.

"Marcus has grown up. What is he around 6 foot, 2 inches? He's kinda cute. I bet you he still has a crush on you."

"Girl, shut up," I lashed out.

After my brief encounter with Marcus, we talked from time to time. It was apparent that he still liked me, but who didn't. I enjoyed his conversations, but Ja'Ron took up a lot of my time. My conversations with Marcus were quite short. Heck, finding time to spend with Tasha became a challenge. For all the hype that surrounded Marcus' name, he never got the big head, which made me wonder if he was putting on a front. I mean no one could be that perfect and if he was, it was a major turn off. Who would want a Mr. Goodietwoshoes.

It's Good to Be Back!
MARCUS

My first week of school had my nerves shot. I was coming into an environment that I was accustomed to, yet the 2 ½ year separation had me questioning the transition. All the fellas at Murray Wright wore their pants hanging to their knees, showing dirty draws. My style was more conservative. How was I going to be received? The girls, man, they were fine. Girls wore clothes tight and right. The ones I thought were cute looked through me as if I was invisible. This wasn't anything I hadn't experienced before. When basketball season rolled around, the expected always happened, they noticed a brotha then. It always worked like that. Lord knows that was far from what I was looking for in a female.

I found myself attending classes that had solid teachers, which was unheard of, according to the talk of suburban people about the inner city schools. My boy Dannie had two classes with me, which made classes interesting. He was a nut. He had a joke for everything and was always trying to cap on people. Yo mama this, yo mama that, Dannie hadn't changed much. Every girl that looked halfway decent, he was on her. He dropped more lines than Bill Gates had cash. D' called me janky once because he noticed I was staring at a girl, but refused to talk to her. "Man, what's up with you? You scared of the honies?" he smirked. I didn't fear rejection. I was more scared of missing my opportunity with Sheyla. Okay, I was a little scared of rejection.

"Hey, baby, you musta fell from heaven because you look like an angel," Dannie whispered with one eyebrow lifted slightly over his shades to a young lady that walked by. She barely acknowledged his presence. "Stun, did you see that stare she gave me. Yeah, she wants me." I just looked at him in disbelief. He couldn't have thought that classless verbiage was working. It took all I had not to laugh at this cat.

It was time for basketball conditioning to prepare us for the season. Coach Thomas moved Dannie up to the varsity basketball squad. We were going to play basketball together again, just like old times. The first game of the season started in December, but the Public School League wouldn't allow me to play until January because they had a rule that stated a transfer student had to attend the current school for at least a whole semester before playing any sport. Before our conditioning practice started, I still had a few minutes to spare to go to the nearby store.

Walking in the halls, I saw Shey for the first time since I'd been back. Fine black hair trickling just above her shoulders, brought out her light hazel eyes. This girl was the total package. Her eyes glared as she spoke and she did it for me all over again. Initially, my plan was to keep it cool and not over do it; being aggressive with her didn't get me anywhere in the past, and I wasn't going to blow it this time. The challenge to win her heart was a true goal of mine. I borrowed some change from Dannie to get my favorite Papaya juice from the corner store. Leaving out, I

Retraced

bumped into Shey again, but this time she was with her girl Tasha. "Shey is your number the same," I asked before stepping out the door. She nodded yes. I called her that night and we kept in touch. I was pretty excited, even after she told me about this new boyfriend she had, Ja'Ron Black. The same cat that hated me from back in the day, the brother of the dude I fought for her. This was going to be interesting.

Ja'Ron consumed her time. She was always busy and eager to get off the phone, just to spend it with Mr. Black. One day while in front of the school, Ja'Ron pulls up in his Bronco. Old dude had no respect, just blowing his horn repeatedly to get Shey's attention and break up our conversation. He looked at me and stared. I stared right back, letting him know that Stun was back. I heard him ask if I was who he thought I was. Before driving off, she waved as he continued to mean mug me.

Feeling her resisting me, I decided to continue with staying low. Basketball season had begun and January was fast approaching. This was my year to make up for the two years I lost in Flint. During December our team played hard and was in every game. Dannie ended up starting and averaging 10 points. I was proud of him. He went from J.V. to varsity to starting. Our team record was 1 win and 2 losses. The anticipation for me to play continued to build. You're talking about pressure, it was on.

Right before my first game, I begged Sheyla to come and she finally agreed. Friday arrived with a bang. Whispers traveled through the entire school. I could hear some of the conversations. The same topic continued to pop up. How was I going to perform? This kind of pressure was unusual for me. Basketball came naturally, but this time I had something to prove. We were playing the best senior player in the state. You guessed it, my old rival from P.A.L. days, Lester Vains. He had had a wonderful career up to this point. He was held back his ninth grade year for not performing in class and he didn't play basketball, but apparently he'd gotten himself together. He was in the running for Michigan's Mr. Basketball. The highest award a basketball player could receive in their respective state. Lester had his choice of Big Ten college basketball teams recruiting him.

We were in warm-ups and the crowd was growing. A full house and everyone was coming to see the showdown of Vains vs. Stunson. Sheyla came strolling in with Ja'Ron. I knew from the beginning he was going to be hatin'. Just like he use to when I was younger. Right before the tip-off, Lester gave me a nod of respect and the game took off. Lester played a very controlled game, showing his maturity, while I got caught in the hype and missed my first six shots. Coach Thomas immediately pulled me aside, "son let the game come to you. Relax, settle down and quit forcing the issue. We all know you can play." I instantly followed his direction. I later scored ten straight points and the crowd began chanting, "Stunson, Stunson, Stunson." I started feeling it and I was just beginning. The night ended with me scoring eight points more than Lester's 30. We won and the crowd rushed the floor. You would've thought it was the playoffs. Everything was good, so I decided not to greet Shey and her apparently disgruntled boyfriend. I didn't need anything negative spoiling the mood. As soon as I dried off from showering, three different newspaper reporters questioned me. Man, the media frenzy was crazy; I wasn't prepared for the hype. With the fight for Mr. Basketball, the media followed Lester to every game, so I should have expected it. The next day the paper read 'THE PILOTS **STUN** VAIN'S PIONEERS,' with a big color picture of me driving to the basket.

The next day I decided to catch the bus down to the Brewster projects, initially to see some old childhood friends, but mostly to see Sheyla and Mrs. Patron. It seemed like an eternity that I knocked. Mrs. Patron opened the door. The simmering sound of fire heating up grease, with a fresh aroma of sausage met me at the door.

"Hey, Mrs. Patron, how you've been?" I asked.

"Oh great and what about yourself. I'm so happy you came back home."

"Yeah, so am I. It was definitely a learning experience," I responded.

"Well, Shey should be down soon. She's in the shower. There's food on the stove, so fix some if you're hungry. Just relax and watch television," Mrs. Patron said motioning me to the couch. Second to my grandmother, she was the nicest lady you could meet. I think she always looked at me as the son she never had. How fitting, especially with my pursuit of Shey's eternal love.

As I turned, her smile made my heart jilt. She had these jeans on that screamed look at me. Her hair just flowed off her shoulders. Man, she was fine. "What brings superstar to my house?" She asked. "Nutt'in, I just wanted to see an old friend. I'm kinda surprised you're not with your man."

"Boy shut up," grinning while she drank a cup of orange juice. "Before yesterday's game did you catch one of your nervous mysterious migraine headaches?"

"What? You trying to be funny, but naw. Not at all. Lately, they've been light. I guess I'm heeled by Jeeesusss," I jokingly said.

Our conversation was warm and inviting. There was no way of denying our friendship. It remained pretty tight through the years. "Hey that garbage is stacked, let me take that out for you." She laughed, "boy you are somethin' else." I began wondering about Ja'Ron. "Hey, it's Saturday, so why aren't you with your man?" She said something about him taking care of business in Ohio. Whenever the Blacks said business, we knew it meant drugs, and she tried to act like she didn't know.

She asked me to walk her to the store to get some bread and butter. While walking we reminisced about the old times. It tripped us out that I grew up down here in the projects, and she visited her grandmother often before moving down here, yet we hadn't met until I moved out of the Brewster's to stay with my Grandmother after my moms murder. Our conversation was non-stop, then I noticed how red her ears were, so I gave her my scarf to wrap around her head. She looked at me saying thanks with her smile. We laughed and joked until we made it back to her door. During our talk, she mentioned how Ja'Ron bought her all the hottest gear and took her to top restaurants, yet in the midst of her bragging, I could see through her. She was unhappy. Something was missing. It made me think back to when she messed around with his brother. "Hey, Shey, has Ja'Ron ever hit you."

"Nooo. And why would you ask that?"

"I'm sorry. I didn't mean to offend you, but I know his type."

"Marcus, you hatin' on my boyfriend?" She asked mockingly.

"No, but on the real, stay safe." I wanted to tell her how much she meant to me. But again, I had to play it cool. As we walked up the stairs, Sheyla slipped and fell right into my arms. She said thanks, as we both stared into the other's soul. She was so soft and fragile. It was nice to see my crush hadn't left. It felt like it matured to a love from afar. "Are you coming in or going to see your friends?" she asked. How could I turn an invitation from Sheyla down. "I guess I will," blushing, trying to hide my excitement. We went inside and straight clowned. I mean talking about when we first met, my experiences in Flint, just enjoying one another's company. Just when we were connecting, her phone rung. "Hey boo! It's good to hear from you. Where are you?" Yeah it was ole' boy. "I guess I'll leave," I whispered, walking towards the door. Sheyla gave me a nod of approval ending our day together.

Monday came around and I was on the prowl to see Sheyla. I checked her usual spots, but she was nowhere around. I thought she was absent, but then I noticed a young flash of a princess rushing out of the building. I called; she ignored me. Finally I caught up to her and noticed she wouldn't look me in my eyes. "Shey, what's wrong? Why are you rushing off?" "No reason, I just need to get home." That's when I noticed at a glance her right eye was dark and puffy. To save her the embarrassment, I refused to ask what happened. There was no need, her swollen eye spoke louder than an echoing choir. Mr. Dope Man was following the family tradition of beating women. "Bye, Shey," flowed from my lips as I turned in a daze of irritation.

That night I popped on the radio, Michael Jackson's old song Human Nature was on. I sang along off key, half messing up the words.

The thought of that clown hitting the girl that captured my heart made me sick to my stomach. But while Stevie Wonder was playing in the background, I decided to make a quick tape of the love songs that I had in my collection. After recording the last song, I spoke some words of love.

"Therapeutic sounds of the voice that speaks to me daily, my heart is entangled in your current dilemma Sheyla,

You shook by a man whose intellect reflects the gold around his neck,

While the essence of genius surface my soul to find your heart and connect. Imagine how our love could be. A house on the hills doesn't explain my dream, that's fine

But without love to establish a home it becomes a fruitless vine

> So unwind to a man of valor, a man of vision
> I present myself to rescue you from your warden and his prison"

Just a little poem to get her thinking. In my head, I could hear Dannie saying how stupid I was, and how I was being too strong. But I just wanted to see what it could lead to.

"Dannie, wake up."

"I'm up. Whatcha need?"

"Can you pick me up and take me over Shey's house?" I asked.

"Dawg, it can't wait until tomorrow?"

"Come on kidd. Forget it, I'll ride my bike over there," I said knowing I wasn't speaking the truth.

"Alright, alright. You lucky you my dawg, I'll be there in ten. Be ready. And Stun, you owe me."

"No doubt," I answered with a sigh of relief.

In the midst of winter, I'm sweating, nervous tremors rippling through my body trying to rehearse what I was going to say to Shey. Annoyance from blank thoughts, my words just wouldn't formulate meaning. Every step towards the outside of her window submerged my feet into a foot of snow. Every breath from my nose pushed out a small smoke cloud, signifying how cold a brotha was. Nothing was going to stop me from talking to her, even if I didn't have the words to explain my purpose for being there.

It was too late for me to ring her doorbell. I decided to find some pebbles to throw at her window. With all the snow around, that was a dumb thought; there were none to be found. Without delay, I broke some branches off a nearby tree and broke them into small parts. It took five tries before finally getting her attention.

There she was, scarf on her head with a shocked look looking as beautiful as ever. "Who is that?" Trying not to

wake up her grandmother, I whispered, "Shey it's me."
"Marcus Stunson is that you out there freezing like a fool?"
"The one and only," I answered.
"You are crazy, boy. Grams will have a fit, even if it is you!"
"I know, but can you come down for sec?"
"Hold on, here I come. Make it quick whatever it is." Before she came downstairs, I still couldn't quite make out what it was I was going to say.

"Shey, first of all I'm sorry for making you feel like I deserved an explanation for your past dealins' with men." Before I could finish she blurted out, "Boy, no problem, really it's okay." "Wait," I interrupted her. "I was thinking about you and wanted to bring you a little somethin' to let you know you'll have my friendship for life." Feeling her staring at me, I began to sing. "You and I, on earth together it's just," I song way off key, breaking the tension. She laughed stopping in the middle of the verse of my favorite Stevie Wonder song. "You are off," laughing at my foolishness. "Just kiddin'," handing her the tape I made and a plastic rose I took off my grandmother's bookcase. Our hands met as she received the gifts. She jerked away and politely said she had to go before her grandmother woke up. Without saying a word, her eyes fought to resist my affection. The tear on the edge of her bottom eyelash said it all.

On my way back home, Dannie had 101 questions, but no answers were required. The look I met him with expressed my confusion as much as his inquiry anticipated. I really didn't know what had really happened. All that mattered was what I hoped I'd accomplished.

SHEYLA......
The game

It was kind of exciting, anticipating Marcus's first game back in Detroit. The whole school was in limbo over what he could do on the court. Known as the one always seeking attention, I was proud to acknowledge Marcus as my little brotha. Knowing I would need a ride to attend the game, I begged Ja'Ron to go. He was so against it at first, which really didn't make sense to me. I knew he liked basketball, so him acting as if I was taking him to an opera was weird. Entering the gym, I saw Marcus and so I whispered good luck. Immediately a sharp nudge from an elbow pierced my side. Ja'Ron looking in frustration, gave me the what's up with that look. I felt jealousy was a way for him to express his love, so it was nice to see him express himself immaturely. With all the respect his presence demanded, he never acted threatened by anyone and out of all people it became apparent to me that Marcus was someone that intimidated him.

Marcus became Stun on the court again. No one could stop this boy, he really had a gift. I was so proud of him. Cheers roared shaking the bleachers. Everyone immediately rushed to get to Marcus. Out of my side view, girls were acting as if he was the hottest thing around. Ja'Ron rushed me out the gym before I could congratulate Marcus on his game. Going home, Ja'Ron refused to talk to me. His jealousy wasn't cute anymore. I hadn't given him a reason to be so out with frustration. "Ja, are you upset with me?" I asked out of curiosity. "I don't know, should I be?" He answered staring me in my eyes with a look to kill. He made me feel so uncomfortable. Getting out of his car, I turned to say good night, but he ignored me and dropped me off without seeing me in the house safely.

The next day, Ja called to say he had bizness to attend to and I shouldn't expect to see him Saturday. He hung up before I could ask any questions. Soon after, Mr. Stun came by. Irritated by Ja'Ron, it was good to see Marcus just to holla at an old friend. He was as silly as ever. Our conversation flowed into a continuation of the last few conversations we had a few years ago. Our friendship was still intact. He wasn't as goofy and his innocence was adorable. Marcus' vulnerability worried me though because his actions towards others were surreal, unequivocally, unadulterated wholesome in nature. While he was visiting, Ja'Ron called and I told him Marcus came by. He immediately dropped his so-called bizness to make sure Marcus had gone. Three hours passed and I got the signal phone call, which meant for me to meet Ja'Ron outside my house. Knowing he was safe away from his dealings in the streets, I greeted him with a big hug. He greeted me with a smack to my face. Whop!! "Slut, who you thank you messin' wit. Ha! Nobody plays me! No whatam sayin." Crying, dazed and confused, I couldn't believe he went off like that. "I don't want to hurt you, but you ain't 'bout to give yo lovin to no other nigga. You feel me." He screamed, got into his car and drove off. Standing in the cold, freezing, I had to sneak back in the house without Grams noticing me bewildered. I ran to the bathroom staring in the mirror into a bankrupt soul. I had seen domestic violence on T.V., but not once did I believe I'd be a candidate for help. Even though no one new the emotional pain I went through, my heart was ashamed of me, retracing the path my mom traveled. With my emotions, there was no way, no will, no desire, no no how of leaving Ja'Ron. It was as if my death would be the only way to separate me from him.

"Sheyla get the phone please!" Grams yelled from the basement. Anticipating it was Ja'Ron with an explanation, I ran to the phone. "Hello." A light voice hesitant, "hey bey, it's your mutha." An anchor attached itself to my heart and fell to my stomach. "Who is this playing games?" "Shey, don't be alarmed. It's me and I don't have a lot of time to talk. We got word that me and T.C. made the news back home."

"Yes, momma! Are you alright? I can't believe it's really you. Whats going on? Did he do something to you? Are you coming home?" I asked rapidly needing every one of my questions answered.

"Baby hold on, I'm thinking about coming home to turn myself in. Momma's so scared. I can't continue to live like this. Hey, here comes T.C. Let me go," she said with great sadness in her voice. When Grams came upstairs, I let her know what was up and she immediately called the police. "Officer, I'm Ms. Patron and my daughter is on the run with a fugitive. She just called my house and I'm asking that you guys trace the call." As the conversation continued, I noticed her smile. "Grams, what did they say," I asked as she threw up her hand for me to hold on. She said the cops had been on moms trail for months already and was confident they'd find her soon. While talking to Grams, I made sure I used my hand and positioned myself to hide my slightly swollen eye.

I wasn't as relieved as she was. If T.C. finds out that my mother brought heat on him, he'd kill her. Going to school with all this drama piled up in my head had me on low-key status. My eye being a little puffy and my mom's safety had me on straight hiatus. Successfully hiding from Tash and the girls, I thought I was in the clear, but right when I was on my way out the door heading home, Marcus noticed me. Not wanting to explain my face, I tried to avoid looking at him. His hand reached out to me. For some strange reason, it represented safety. His eyes possessed an air of compassion that left me confused on what that moment meant. Why was I feeling like Lois Lane talking to Superman. There was shelter in his presence. The moment was strange and I guess in my split second of emotional distress that encounter had me trippin'. Oh well. That night I stayed to myself. I didn't accept any phone calls, just searching for peace of mind. While dozing off for the night, I heard this pecking sound against my window.

As I looked down to see who it was, the darkness of night covered their face and I could only make out that it was some guy. Then a voice spoke with a familiar resonance. It was Marcus being the charmer he was, standing there begging me to come downstairs. My grandmother would've killed both of us, but I was interested in knowing why he came so late and couldn't wait to see me in school the next morning. His words were so wholesome. I felt honored to have such a friend in my life.

I guess I needed the company because I wasn't shooing him away like I should have done, especially knowing the drama he caused between Ja'Ron and I. We kicked it for a minute with his silly self then he handed me a cassette tape and a plastic rose. How sweet. With all the rejections, this guy was a friend and still pursuing me. I wished I could offer him more, but I couldn't. He was just lil' ole' Marcus. Tears began to form and holding back my sensitivity was hard, so I decided to go back in the house. I rushed to get the tape recorder to listen to what was on the tape. Lying down, it hit me. His cologne drifted from each leave of the plastic rose into my nostril. Listening to the tape put me in a silence of total appreciation. Every song recorded had deep meaning and was a favorite. The tape had real words expressing true love on it. At the end of the tape, Marcus whispered in the mic a sweet poem that made me blush. Again, I felt this warm welcoming feeling I had about him some years ago, but in a more mature way. I was more appreciative of who he was now; he was a very caring and giving of himself.

The next day I talked to Dannie, he told me Marcus wasn't in school. Disappointment arose after he staying home with a migraine cancelled the expectancy of me seeing his face. I wanted to thank Marcus for lifting my spirits at a time when I was feeling pretty low, so as soon as I got home, I called him. "Hey, is this Marcus?" I asked.

"Yeah, it's me, who dis?"

"Boy, it's Shey. I'm just calling to thank you for last night and to see how you were doing."

"I'm straight. My head was killing me and I just needed to rest my body, so my grandmother let me stay home."

"Well, let me go so you can rest. I just wanted to holla at you for a minute."

"Kidd, hearing your voice alone has made me feel better, so don't ever think you have to rush off the phone with me. But it's cool if you gotta go. Wait, hold up. On Sunday, we're having friends and family day at my grandmother's church; it would be nice to see you there." While I concentrated on his gentle soul, a long pause followed between he and I before I said goodbye. I wish I had the ability to put Marcus's spirit into Ja'Ron's body. His gentleness met me right when I needed it most.

I rushed home anticipating Ja'Ron's call. After his weekend business trips, he usually called me at a routine time. Opening my front door, I saw my grandmother looking bewildered. She looked straight through me while grabbing her left side. The phone was knocked over on the side of the couch loudly blaring the-off-the hook-sound. Grams was in trouble, fighting to get help. I immediately picked up the phone and dialed 911. "Hello, operator, I need someone here right away! I think my grandmother is having a heart attack!" I threw the phone down and ran to her side. Her eyes rolled to the back of her head and scared me into a panic. I dashed to the kitchen to grab a rag and submerged it in dishwater. Me rubbing the rag over her perspiring head gave her little relief if any. "Grams, I'm here. It's going to be all right. It will, I know it will," I spoke softly as I sat on the floor caressing her stiff body. The fear of death would send anyone into prayer.

"Lord, please heal my grandmother. She's all I have. Don't let her die. PLEASE!

Grams, I'm sorry for my behavior. I'll change, just don't leave me." Her breath turned to moans of pain. I questioned the amount of time it took for the ambulance to arrive; every lapsed minute seemed like an hour and just a second closer to my grandmother's demise. Finally, I heard the ambulance pull up in the parking lot. Paramedics came in and went right to work. Not giving them an opportunity to make a mistake, I got out of the way and watched every move they made as we headed to the hospital.

I felt like a part of me was dying. My mouth hung open in shock, as I thought about life without the woman who loved me in spite of my vile behavior. "Young lady, are you okay? Don't worry, your grandmother will be just fine," one of the paramedics remarked after noticing me in shock and trying to get me to settle down.

Waiting in the lobby was unbearable. I decided to call the only person that Grams would've called in a time of need. Ms. Caroline picked up the call on the first ring and before I could finish telling her everything that happened,

Retraced

she hung up and was on her way. Ms. Caroline rushed through the doors with Marcus following and calmed my nerves some. Physically tired and emotionally depleted, I fell into Marcus's arms crying on his shoulder. Ms. Caroline grabbed both of us and erupted into prayer for the Lord to heal my grandmother and to make me strong. Marcus and I didn't speak. We sat down and I rested my head on his shoulders. Even without saying a word, he was so comforting. He put his right arm over my shoulders, gently caressed my arm; and held me with such tenderness. I felt so guilty because he was always there for me and I hadn't reciprocated that kind of loyalty to him. Immediately, the Doc came out with a stern face.

"Hi, Sheyla, I'm your grandmother's doctor, Dr. Hetoff. We discovered your grandmother suffered a slight heart attack, due to an unstable angina. We gave her an angiogram, after which we placed a balloon catheter in her blood vessel to create a space for us to put a stent in the vessel. The stent creates a broader opening in the vessel so the blood will flow through; this should prevent any future blockage. It was an in and out process, which went very well; she'll be out of here in a day or two. Any questions, Sheyla?"

"No Doc., not at all," I answered.

"Good. I'm prescribing your grandmother some medication, Heparin, that she'll need to take daily. Oh, and Sheyla keep her away from stress. Don't worry her, she'll be fine."

"Thanks, Doc. You've been very helpful," I responded.

"Hallelujah, thank yaaa!" Ms. Caroline screamed at the top of her lungs. Poor Marcus, if he wasn't embarrassed, I was embarrassed enough for the both of us. We all just looked at her as she hollered, jumped around and sung hymns. Everyone in the waiting room stared, some even with their mouths all twisted. One doctor even came out to ask if everything was okay.

"Shey, you need some rest, we'll take you home," Ms.

Caroline suggested. Outside, Marcus wrapped his scarf around me as we walked out. I saw Ja'Ron's boy, Tone, bringing some girl to the hospital. I couldn't let him see me. If word got back to Ja'Ron about me and Marcus being together again, Ja would act a fool. Reflexes and fear took over and I, without thinking, pushed Marcus away. "Yo, what's up wit that? I'm here for you, but you be trippin'," a puzzled Marcus responded. "I'm sorry, I just need to get home and rest. I'm very tired," I said.

Grams was eager to get home, but at the last minute the doctors decided to hold her over for two days for more observations. We were scheduled to pick her up on Sunday afternoon. In the meantime, I decided to go to Ms. Caroline's church.

On Sunday, Ms. Caroline and Marcus picked me up for church. I felt like I was walking the carpet of a king's castle. The church was beautiful. Every square foot of the sanctuary was covered with red rosy carpet. When we walked into the plush cathedral, ushers welcoming us to worship immediately greeted us. Man, this getup had a whole different feel to it; instead of devotion, this church kicked it off with praise and worship. I could really feel something stirring in the atmosphere. It was spooky because I hadn't experienced church like this before. Everyone was so nice. The pastor preached 'Hell is Real'. This was the first time I had enjoyed church from beginning to end. "Ms. Caroline is church always like this?" I asked. "Oh yeah, baby. The anointing is here every Sunday," she answered. I swear church with my Grams wouldn't have been so bad had Gram's church been like this one.

On the way to pick up my grandmother, I noticed Marcus said little of nothing. He finally showed signs of being a real person with this somber mood. He wasn't Marcus, Mr. Perfect. I wanted to know what was going on with him, but he wouldn't look at me. "Marcus, how did you enjoy church today," I asked. "It was straight, Pastor Morwood was cool."

Instead of being a nuisance, harassing him about his attitude, I just left it alone for a minute.

After church, we picked Grams up. Her sedated, lifeless body made it hard to transport her from room to room. Marcus helped me walk Grams in the house and up to her bedroom. Walking back downstairs, I pulled him to the side and gave it one last go. "Marcus are you sure you're alright," I stared in his eyes, forcing him to commit to an answer.

"Shey, you know what, I'm just tired of you being up one minute then down another. hollering at me when it's convenient for you. You just don't get it.

"Get what Marcus?" I asked.

"I'm in love with you!" Marcus said. A long pause caused us to gape motionless until I gathered my thoughts.

"Marcus, I'm sorry, but I never led you on. We've been friends for years, why trip now?"

"Kid, you know what, you're right. I've been a fool this whole time. Yo, I'll holla at you later," Marcus turned his back and rushed out of the door.

"Wait, wait, wait a minute." Marcus continued walking, ignoring my attempt to explain that my words may have been too harsh.

His words, "I'm in love with you," replayed in my head and it made me analyze my own feelings. I mean being around him always made me happy, and I always welcomed his warmth, his comfort, well maybe. Naw, it wasn't there, or at least not enough to respond with I love you too, let's date. What made him love me so? Right after this little drama with Marcus, Ja'Ron called.

"What up, Shey, I've been trying to reach you all day."

"Ja, my grandmother was rushed to the hospital this week, and I decided to go to church today, so I've been tied up."

"Is she still living?" He giggled.

"Ja, do you think I'd be this calm if she was dead or close to it! The Lord saved her," I responded, very irritated by his question and action.

"The Lord! You Ms. Churchy girl now," Jaron laughed, ignoring my feelings.

"Anyways. When do I get to see you Ja?"

"I'll be in Detroit tonight. I'll see you then or tomorrow. Let me go."

"I love you Ja'Ron."

"Yeah, me too," Ja'Ron said.

After speaking to Ja'Ron, I could understand Marcus feeling of frustrated love. I was becoming increasingly discouraged and upset with Ja'Ron's antics. Him spending all this time out of town had me convinced he was with another girl. That night Ja'Ron came over while Grams was resting. Ja'Ron pressed the issue for me to give up my goods. I hadn't seen nor had I heard from him and he wanted to come over, sex me up and be out. He didn't say, baby I'm sorry, I missed you. He didn't even buy me anything. "So what's up, did you see your little boyfriend today?" He asked.

"Now what are you talking about? What boyfriend?"

"You know, little Marcus," Ja'Ron smirked testing my patience.

"See you trippin' again. What's that all about? You are my man! I just want you to act like it. Anyway, what's up with you and Marcus. Why do you hate him so?" I screamed expressing my annoyance with his immaturity.

"Oh, you taking up for him now. He's a little punk, that's all. Besides, why are you all on his jock. Let's see, maybe because he hoops. Why you always hangin' around this dude is the question?" Ja'Ron said in an uproar.

I had to pause to collect my thoughts. I felt like he was being so insensitive. "Ja'Ron, do you remember the infamous Brewster murder from back in the day," I asked.

"Yeah, fa sho. It was brutal, but I'm sho well deserved too."

"Boy, YOOOU ARRRE CRAZY! The lady that was killed was Marcus's mom and he witnessed the whole thing."

"You mean he was there and saw everything?" he asked.

"Exactly."

"So what does that have to do with me? And if he had, why didn't he go to the police?"

"Ja, I don't know all the ins and outs, but he witnessed a murder and so did I. He doesn't have his mom and neither do I. Can't you see? All we are are friends with a lot in common, that's it," I pleaded trying to get Ja'Ron to finally empathize and understand my friendship with Marcus. I was for sure this would end all the extra tension, but it didn't. He continued to say I was using any reason to be around Marcus. I just gave up and refused to mention Marcus' name again.

After our brief exchange, he was off again. He was so busy. I often wondered what was he thinking. The affection wasn't passionate; he was unconcerned with what I was going through with my Grams and he never asked anything about my mother. Our relationship was becoming fruitless and it troubled me. Was his desire to get money pushing him to the brink of corruption and despair? If so, would it take me with him?

I had to be strong for my Grams so I couldn't let my domestic turbulence be the catalyst for her stress to increase. She meant much more to me than that. Finding out I was deeply involved, infatuated, and in love with a guy who threatened my existence every time we hung out would send her right back into the hospital.

"Shey, Shey, come here baby," Grams called out. "Yes, Grams. What is it?" Helplessly looking in my direction she said, "baby, who was that downstairs? Was that still Marcus?" "Ah, yes grams, it was. Yeah that was Marcus who just left."

Marcus name brought up the fact that I needed to soothe things over with him. I knew I hurt him.

The next day in school I noticed that Marcus wasn't hanging in his usual spots. I still wanted to apologize for the way my words came out the previous day. He didn't deserve it and besides Tasha, he was someone I could truly call a friend. I guess you can say I genuinely was concerned about Marcus Stunson. Towards the end of the day I met him at a class I knew he attended consistently. "Hey, Marcus, how are you?" He looked and smiled, "doing good, just ready to get this day over with. Good seeing you, but I can't be late for this class. Gotta go." He rushed into the room before I could finish my thought.

After talking to Marcus, Ree Ree rushed up to me. Ree Ree was a girl that tried to hang out with me and Tash sometimes. She was a hoodrat. Due to her shiestiness and willingness to sleep with any dude that approached her, she would've given our crew a bad name, so I tried to keep my distance. Ree was so foul about herself that she even made my girl Tasha look like an angel. "Shey, hold on. I need to talk to you." With her, it was always drama so I answered reluctantly. "I know you and Marcus are cool. You think you can put a good word in for a sista?" First thing that popped in my head was NO WAY! Marcus wouldn't even give a girl like Ree Ree a second thought. Plus he was too good for her. Grudgingly I said, "well yeah. I'll uh, I'll talk to him. Alright." She walked off with a big grin that shows the diamond she had glued to her front tooth. What was I thinking? The day ended before I could relay the message.

Days went by before Ree Ree asked whether I'd talked to Marcus about her new found crush. It slipped my mind, but I knew it didn't matter because she didn't have a standing chance. "Sorry, Ree; I forgot." Displeasure was written all over her face. "You know what, that's cool. I'll holla at him myself," she responded and walked away with much attitude. The week continued with Marcus avoiding me. I tried to pretend that I wasn't bothered by his pettiness, but there was no way to deny I needed his conversation, his care, his company.

"What's up, Shey. John is taking me home today. Do you need a ride?"

"I do. Thanks, Tasha," I answered walking out the door noticing Marcus and Ree Ree walking in the hallway side by side. "Well, aren't you going to say bye to your homeboy," Tasha asked. "Girl, naw. I'll let him spend time with Little Ms. Hoochie Momma over there."

"Ah ha! Do I detect a little jealousy Ms. Sheyla Patron?"

"Girl, please. You know me betta than that." The attention he usually gave me was being absorbed by some hoodrat chickenhead caught up in basketball hysteria. The frustration mounted when I stood waiting by the phone and Ja'Ron never called, which was becoming a habit. He usually had a check in time, but now he called sporadically, whenever he felt like it. Tasha didn't call and I began to think that Marcus was even starting to get caught up in his own hype because he didn't call either. This Friday was a complete bore with nobody to talk to. Hmmph, the sexiest girl in Murray Wright and I was at home fed up with feeling under appreciated.

Grams was starting to get stronger and about her everyday business, which included reverting to her old ways; being her own private investigator concerning me. I was trying to stay out of her hair to alleviate any possible stress, but it's like she wasn't happy unless she was able to fuss at me. I mean, she did a complete 360 degrees right back into the lady that made my life a living hell. "Shey, I'm tired of one of your little friends calling and hanging up in my face. Do you know who it might be?" First thing I thought about was Ja'Ron's secret call to let me know that he was either around the corner or wanting me to call him back. "How many times did they call?" I asked. "Let me see, once when I was praying, another time when I was cooking, and one mo time when I was washing clothes. I would say three or four times. Why! Do you know the person playing on the phone like that?" She just kept digging and digging. I was so frustrated. I just needed to get out of the house, so I called Tasha to see if she had her boyfriend's car.

Tasha picked me up about an hour later. Grams demanded that I was to be in by ten o'clock, but after begging and pleading, I got Grams to agree to 11:30 p.m. on a Friday night. I thought I was grown, which made Grams' strictness despicable. Tash and I rode around seeing what we could get into. We decided to go downtown to the Renaissance Center and to GreekTown. All of the top Greek restaurants were in Downtown Detroit-in Greektown. Most of our friends hung out at Pizza Plaza, because it was the main hangout spot for most high school students in our area. Anybody who was a somebody gravitated to this joint on Friday nights. It also was the pick up spot for older guys to find young girls they could turn out. In fact this is where my girl Tash finds most of her male friends.

Towards the back of the restaurant, we heard a lot of ruckus. Kids were wearing red and blue, screaming Northern High School. Someone from the school knew Tash from somewhere and said "Hey, y'all, they're from Murray." Suddenly all the attention shifted directly toward us. "We're going to kill the Pilots," roared from the lips of the rowdy crowd. We sat down to order when the girl that knew Tash sat next to her, escorted by some tall dude wearing a red and blue varsity jacket. His face was covered with pimples and his body was immersed in foul cologne. Tasha's eyebrows pressing towards the center of her forehead couldn't make out who these people were. "Hey ladies, do y'all know Marcus Stunson?" The girl asked.

"Yeah we know him, she knows him betta," Tash said

pointing to me. The tall dude staring at me interrupted and proceeded to sit down next to me. "Yo, let me holla atcha for a second. What's yo name and can I get those digits?" he asked.

"None of your biz wacks and no you can't! Does that answer your questions?" He immediately stood up after my rejection and introduced himself.

"Well, my name is Jacobi Wright. Y'all boy went for 40 points the last time we played him. I was hurt and didn't play, so let him know it's on and poppin' the next game," he said and walked away. The girl that Tash hadn't identified stayed back. "Since you know Marcus, give him this number for me." She handed me a napkin with the name Candie and her phone number written on it. She walked away and all I could think about was how much of an airhead she was; she was like a black version of a dumb blonde. Candie, I thought, "Tash, her name was Candie. Does that ring a bell?" Tash looked puzzled and said "Not at all." I tore the phone number up in pieces.

After finishing our food, we went to the Renaissance Center to walk around. Kickin' it with Tash, I heard Ree Ree's voice in back of me. It was Ree Ree and MARCUS. "What up Ree and Marcus," I greeted. "Girl, I thought that was y'all," Ree Ree answered.

"So, you ain't going to speak Marcus," I asked.

"I was just waiting on you and Ree to finish your dialogue. Naw, but what's up ladies?"

"We just saw some dude that plays for Northern say he was going to kill you. I think his name was Jacobi something," I said.

"Straight up. That dude don't really want to see me on the court," Marcus replied.

Tasha stared at me as if she could see my irritation with this little gathering. Marcus looked lost and uncomfortable standing in the background, barely interacting. It felt like someone had turned up the heat, boiling my blood to the point of blowing off the rooftop. Why was I so heated? I mean Marcus wasn't my man. Ree Ree ain't a real friend and Marcus has every right to date and not answer my every beck and call. That was reasonable thinking, but my mind at the time wasn't thinking reasonably by any means. "Let's go girl," Tash urged me to leave, knowing I was just a little fired up.

Before leaving, a little white kid ran up to Marcus, "Stun, Stun, can I have your autograph?" The little boy's mother ran to grab him, "Sorry, Marcus. My son knows all about Detroit basketball, and he has cut outs and News article clippings of you all on his wall. He says everyday, he's going to play like you because you're one of the top players in the country." Marcus, being so compassionate, reached to hug the boy and signed his name on the hat he was wearing. Today, I witnessed the magnetism Marcus had on people. What everyone else saw in him, that gleam of pure light, his heart and soul made me appreciate what I had previous ignored. He wore his heart on his sleeve embracing every second of Gods oxygen with love. Yet I sat back taking advantage of his devotion, turning a friend into an enemy. He was no longer there for me. Self-indulgence was the complete representation of who I was and what I stood for. After seeing how happy Ree Ree was in Marcus's presence, I pulled Tash to the side and urged her to take me home. Enough was enough.

"Girl what is up with you," Tash asked

"Nothing! I'm just ready to get home. I need to talk to Ja'Ron and check on grams."

"Shey, there you go playing games. You're upset cause yo' boy got himself a girl and you miss him jockin' you, treating you like a queen. That's selfish. Let the boy move on. You know you don't really want him. Or at least want him for the right reasons."

For a girl who always had a sermon to preach, she sure didn't listen to her own messages. She confused me sometimes because with her mouth she could be the President, but with her actions she could be quite embarrassing. I mean after dropping me off, she was going to prepare to strip at some after-hours joint. Even still, she had a point and she knew me, so I took heed to her words.

Our Junior year was coming to an end and our friendship wasn't the same. Marcus would call every now and then, but it wasn't the same conversations. My pride wouldn't allow me to let him know that I missed the vibe and connection we shared for years. Between all of his fans and basketball, I was third in line. Not having the friend to depend on exposed how bothered I was becoming with Ja'Ron. Ja'Ron started getting more money, spending more time away, and at the same time becoming more possessive. He sexed me up like no other could, which kept me dependent. I began looking forward and accepting the short nights with him, but there was so much missing, and I was displeased at what I was becoming. Truth be told, I think I fell in love with the idea of someone loving me the way Marcus did. So I let things remain.

Who Is This That They Call ME???
MARCUS......

What if Shey lost her grandmother? My heart went out to her in a way that only one that has experienced a deep tremendous lost can. As soon as my grandmother said Ms. Patron was in the hospital, I needed to be there for the Sheyla, queen of my heart. Entering the waiting room, seeing her eyes retrieve from chaos to relief was a needed feeling. It was like her night and shining armor came through for her. She fell into my arms, where I could do nothing but caress her. For the first time I'd seen a sign of vulnerability. She always kept this tough exterior in front of me, but the sensitive Shey was even more attractive. During this time, we hugged and caressed as I walked her to the car. Some cat that looked like the typical, I want to be a gangster, walked past, and she immediately played me off. As if she didn't want homeboy to see her hugged up with me. With all the emotional trauma she'd been through, she was able to pull herself together for the attention of some dude I doubt she knew. The more I hung around her, I understood how much of a fool I really was. Fighting for her love was a battle I'd lost.

That Sunday we picked Shey up to go to church with us. Even though she was fly as ever, my anger wasn't caving in on this one. "Hey Marcus." Sheyla spoke.

"Oh. What's up?"

"Boy you know you sharp!"

I looked in the opposite direction, acting like she hadn't said anything and turned up the car stereo.

Even though I presented myself as a guy that had it all together, I was really fighting an emotional war within. Basketball was no longer the remedy for personal distress. In Flint, basketball betrayed me. The girl I've loved for years betrayed my affection. The system of justice failed my mother and I. The older I became, the more cynical I became, and I was finally starting to deal with hidden issues that were subconsciously tearing me up inside.

In school, coaches expected one thing from me, teachers looked at me as the ideal student, and colleges had even gotten into the mix. With all the pressures, I had to present this good boy image, yet my anger grew as I developed into a young man. I had gotten to a point where I no longer understood myself.

The so-called Brewster murder was the label attached to the memory of my beloved mother's death. Her murder haunted me, which made me grieve the most. What was once something I tried to ignore, continued to confront me. With the success I was having on the basketball court, I wanted someone to share it with the way my teammates did. The mother's of our team were very involved with their sons. After one game, I sat on the bench to see who would greet me. My teammates were congratulated by their parents, but I stood off invisible to everyone but the little groupie girls. My grandmother wasn't that involved in sports, and she was kinda old school; the stay-at-home, cook and go to church type. She really didn't attend my games. My grandmother loved me tremendously, but it couldn't replace a mother's love.

The more I focused on not having a mom, the more her murder stayed at the forefront of my mind. The murderer for all I knew was roaming around free, yet I was forever imprisoned.

That Sunday we picked up and dropped Shey's grandmother at home. After getting her set to rest, Shey pulled me aside to confront me about my attitude. I ended up telling her that I loved her. Something she knew, but I guess she had to put it to rest this time because she sure let a brotha know that I didn't have a chance. As she talked, my thoughts went to nothing. I gazed at her lips, knowing they would never be kissed by my lips; I felt dejected. Although I had said before that I was done with Shey, this time in my heart I really was ready to move on.

The best way to get over someone is to give it time and space. I made sure during school, I changed my everyday routine so I wouldn't run into her smile, hear her voice, or have to confront my love daily. The few times I saw her; I tried to keep our small talk very small. I knew she wanted to kick it, but she was spoiled. Treating me like I was Burger King, having her way. My boy Dannie was all about helping a brotha out, but I felt he needed help more than I did. His b-boy attitude wasn't working for him, but at least he had the confidence to talk to girls. One would think that it would be easy for a star ball player, but maybe I was too quiet. A shock to me, this girl named Ree Ree approached me though. "Hey, Stun, you played a good game last week. Your handles were straight murder," licking her lips as she squinted her eyes. "What! You know a little about ball."

"Yeah, I do. I also know a lot about you," looking directly in my eyes.

Ree Ree wasn't my ideal girl. I mean, don't get it

twisted, she was an okay looking girl, but her body was on another dimension. She stood 5 feet 7, her hips were thrillers. J-Lo had nothing on Ree. She stood with her back straight up with every step a complete replica of a stallion trotting through the hallways. Her body demanded an audience no matter where she went. The problem was she had a reputation. Walking the halls with her automatically sparked rumors because her rep was scandalous.

"What do you know about me?" I asked enjoying the attention.

"You're the best baller in the state and you only a junior. You got hundreds of colleges vying for you to attend their schools. Oh trust me, I know." I was very impressed. A girl who knew hoops, and she caught me when I was feeling a little down with the Sheyla situation. Why not at least just kick it? She asked to hang out that weekend and I was with it.

Our conversations during the week were cool. She was entertaining and smarter than I expected. That weekend she came to pick me up. Lord knows I didn't expect to see what I saw. Ree Ree had a skirt that barely came down thigh level, tight as can be. She wore a half shirt with her 36 C's exposed. The sight was nice, but I couldn't let her meet my grandmother looking like that. She was trippin' for that one. "Boy, let me see you befo you leave outta here."

"Grams I'm sorry, we'll be late, gotta go," I yelled pushing Ree Ree out the door. "Grandma, I'll be back before twelve." I just wasn't ready for her to see that sight.

We went downtown to the movies at the Renaissance Center. Attention instantly gravitated our way. Old ladies, little kids, all the fellas, and even their dates gave us double and triple dipple stares. I was straight embarrassed. The wind flew left to right, thrown by every move Ree Ree's hips made. Right then and there I knew just why I didn't date those kind of girls. Then she had guys coming up to us. And the girl knew all of them. Sweat started to pour from my head. I didn't go to the stands to buy candy or anything. After getting our tickets, I rushed her right into the theatre to the dark, to get away from all the attention.

Before leaving the Ren Cen, we met up with Sheyla and Tasha. The situation was altogether too much. I stood back hoping we would say hi and by; but Shey wanted to converse. She was looking frustrated, but who knew why. While we were all talking, a little kid ran up to me. His eyes were so innocent and he was excited to meet me. This put a positive light on a day that wasn't going so well. After he asked for my autograph, I obliged; his mom grabbed him, looked at me and then looked at Ree Ree with somewhat of a disappointed look. It made me understand how important my image was too me, and to where I was trying to go in my career. Having a girl who was out like that really wasn't my thing. "So, did you enjoy yourself?" Ree asked.

"Yeah, it was cool. Just next time can you cover up a little," struggling to get the words out of my mouth. "For you, anything," as she grabbed me and gave me a soft kiss on the lips. Just blunt and out from nowhere she asked me was I a virgin. Ree Ree was something else. "Yeah I am," I said without embarrassment.

"Well, we need to take care of that now don't we" pressing her body against mine. My physical reserve was about to scream yes, but I couldn't lead her on. "Ree let's take things slow. We're just friends, and I ain't into using beautiful black queens like that," putting her down lightly, and at the same time subliminally feeding her a message of self-respect. "Marcus, I've never met a boy like you. It's Sheyla isn't it? You guys are more than friends. I seen it in her eyes tonight."

"Naw, we're just friends. I care for her deeply, but naw it ain't like that at all." She accepted what I said, turned off her aggressiveness and walked away blowing me a kiss. Before entering my home, I took a minute to compose. Ree had just taken me on a roller coaster ride.

Retraced

The next day I decided to call coach, just to get some wisdom. Making wise decisions concerning girls and everything else wasn't my forte. Outside of basketball, I hadn't really talked to him. He had an open door policy for us to talk, but I thought I had gotten everything intact and didn't need direction. I ended up meeting him after church. Coach picked me up from our services. "What's going on son? What's troubling you?" He asked.

"Everything, coach." I ended up telling him all of my problems. He let me know how he failed as a husband to his ex-wife and it wasn't until she left him that he found the Lord. "Marcus, it sometimes take trying times for God to get our attention. Especially when you've ignored him. Prayer changes things. Seek the Lord and He will direct your path." He often said similar things that my grandmother would've said, but coming from someone who had similar experiences, his words hit me differently. He was once a star ball player and knew all the hurdles and hassles. "Look Marcus, don't let basketball control you, you control it; stay away from the groupies; make sure your friends are good people and not jeopardizing your career. And as far as your mother's tragic murder, I'll help you in trying to get justice, if you want me to. Son, I'm here for you. Just stay grounded and focused. Seek Jesus Christ."

I decided to really give this Jesus thing a real try. The next Sunday I joined my grandmother's church. She was so proud. That moment even brought us closer. It was beautiful. I stood up and even started to tear a little when I went up front to accept Jesus as my personal savior. It was like his presence was there, saying I'm with you. I didn't really understand what was going on, but it felt right.

Everything felt different. I was free from my mental fights. It wasn't like I no longer had the problems; it was just that I had left them for the Lord to deal with, while I continued with life. All I could do was be me and not let things take me under.

After the date I went on with Ree Ree, she and I ended up being just cool. I made it apparent that she wasn't the one for me. Our little encounter stirred a minor change in her, even though she started messing around with one of my teammates. Her walk toned down and her clothes weren't as revealing as they once were. I was still searching for that special someone, but it was time for me to focus more on basketball. Basketball had to move to the forefront of everything because everyone was gunning to knock down my reputation in hoops.

I had several major college scouts coming to check out our big game in the state championship against Jacobi Wright and the Northern Jayhawks. Michigan, Kansas, Missouri, and Duke made their presence known. I knew exactly where they sat, and I was about to give them the show they were expecting. I knew Jacobi was going to try to show off, so I was going to use that against him. I played off of him to give him the comfort level to just score. He did, falling right into my trap. He scored the first 10 points for his team. I just played a controlled game. Dishing assists, getting steals, and rebounding. Ten minutes into the game I had only scored 4 points, but I had 6 assists, 3 steals, and 7 rebounds, just dominating all aspects of the game. Jacobi ended up shooting erratically because I tightened up the defense and he couldn't score. He became frustrated and started taking all kind of bad shots, taking his team completely out of the flow of their game plan. He missed the next 10 shots, and was taken out the game by his coach. The game started to take a nosedive for us when Dannie got hurt, and Northern had an unsuspecting player light it up. John Springs hit three straight three pointers. The game was out of reach. We lost by 8 points with Jacobi fouling out the game with 15 points. I had a triple double, which should have been reason for celebration, but we lost. Looking at their team celebrate had my blood on straight boil. My teammates were smiling afterwards as if we hadn't lost. It tripped me out, because it seemed as if I was the only one devastated. While parents and girlfriends were greeting my teammates, there I was the star of the show again dealing with the lost alone; no one to lift my spirits. I didn't even shower. I just rushed out of the arena catching a ride with a classmate before the press could get to me.

That summer I was ranked as one of the top 10 seniors in the entire country. I was the favorite for Mr. Basketball in Michigan. Basketball had me traveling from state to state playing in the top summer camps. One camp I attended was the ABCD camp where high school basketball players from all over the country played. The coaches and instructors had classes that educated us on how to deal with all the pressures of being star athletes. My favorite topic was on "What to Expect this Senior Year." I hadn't signed with a university yet and there were magazine articles and news reports that quoted me signing with the North Carolina Tarheels. That information didn't come from me, because I was still unsure. Months had passed and our season was about to begin. Everyone was still speculating on what school I would attend.

Coach had set this scrimmage up with a high school team in Cleveland, Ohio. They were ranked 2nd in the nation, we were ranked 18th in the country. Heading home after we lost the game by two points, we stopped at McDonalds down the street from the campus where we played. After I purchased my food, A face appeared. Boom-boom, bullets echoed throughout the room, hitting my mom as she dropped to the floor. This face standing over her lifeless body stuck in my brain for years. Reliving the worst night of my life, this guy looked like an older version of that picture. I wasn't 100% sure, but I swore this fool was him. He slowly glanced at me with a stare of intimidation. I bumped into my coach as I backed up heading towards the bus. "Marcus what's wrong? What's wrong?" Coach asked. I couldn't respond; complete shock seized the moment. What should be my response? What if this cat wasn't the right guy? Maybe my mind was just trippin'. I just went on the bus shaken. With his imagery embedded in my head, I stepped off the bus for one last look, watching his every move; thinking he could really be my mother's murderer. On our way back home, my teammates were trying to spark a conversation, but my head was gone. Homeboy's face wouldn't leave. This eerie feeling had me.

How Could it Be?
SHEYLA

❧

Months passed with me giving Marcus space. He'd call every now and then to see how my grandmother was doing. His conversations with her were much more in-depth than what he and I spoke about. "Girl, Marcus is a very nice young man. The Lord is really moving in his life. It's good to see young people living for the Lord." Grams sang his praise, as she passed through our narrow hallway trying to entice me to get more involved in church. My thing was, I didn't want to go to church on a just-because notion. I really wanted to feel what my Grams felt, what she saw and heard. Hearing about Marcus and this big moral commitment was trippin' me out. He was a good person and all, but he had this developing recognition with basketball. How could anyone uphold this being saved thing without giving up so much?

I paged Ja'Ron, and he called me right back. "What a surprise," I smiled at the sound of his voice. "What? What are you talking about?" Ja'Ron nervously responded like he was into some foolishness.

"Nothing. I'm just surprised you called right back. I called to see if you would go to church with me this Sunday."

"Not a chance in hell!" His response shocked me. "Ja'Ron, a gentle no would've been fine," I screamed.

"Shey, I didn't mean it like that, but I got some major things coming up. Church is straight up boring anyways. Besides what's up in yo head? This church thing has been a big topic for you lately. You ain't planning on holding back that twa- twa I love so much, are you?"

"Boy, is that all you think about? Is that all I am to you? We don't even hang out like we used to. Bye, Ja'Ron!"

"Baby hold on, it ain't like that. I'm out here in the streets getting this paper, you feel me; if I don't, somebody else will. Get that in yo head and get off my back."

"Bye, Ja'Ron." I hung up. It was confirmed how much our relationship had been at a stand still.

That Sunday Tash and I went to Ms. Caroline's church. It took me a good hour to beg Tash to get out of bed. I couldn't wait to see Marcus face; witnessing me attend his church without him begging would've made his day. All through service, Tasha was squirming, seeming very irritated with sitting for the few hours we spent. "What's wrong, you got ants in your pants," I whispered in her ear. Her eyebrows lifting up in her forehead and her gesturing towards the door gave me the signal she was ready to leave. It was crazy, while I'm enjoying service, she's thinking about how she can make the next dollar. Ms. Caroline met us in the hallway as we left. "Hi, Shey, glad you could make it. Why are you leaving so soon?" She asked. "Well, I came with Tasha and she needs to return her boyfriend's car. By the way, where is Marcus?"

"He's in Ohio with the team. He should be back this evening."

Before Tasha dropped me off, we stopped at the gas station to pick up some snacks. There was Marcus, his face was plastered on the cover of a Sports Illustrated magazine; his smile sent tremors through my heart. 'Stunned With

Skills,' the headline read. I was so proud of him. "Tasha look. Look at my boy," I screamed like I was outside. "Girl I'm right here. Aw snaps, look at yo boy. He blowing up. They got'em looking fly too," Tasha looked me in my eyes waiting for me to react. "Y'all know him personally?" a young looking cashier asked. "Yeah girl, me and Marcus are real close," I said.

"A lot of customers been buyin' that magazine talkin' about that boy. Is he going to the NBA or to college?" She asked.

"We talk all the time, but I ain't sure on that one. I'll get back witcha on that," I answered, blushing with pride. I bought two magazines. Tasha just looked at me. "Girl you sure got hyped when she asked if you knew him. What's up wit that?

Tasha, girl please. I was just answering her questions."

The Article covered Marcus' life from his mom's murder to his upbringing on through to his basketball scandal in Flint. It also talked about how he became a better person after meeting Coach Thomas. It was a very intriguing article that even enlightened me on a few things about Marcus. His mother's death continued to haunt him much deeper than I knew. They pressed him on what college he was going to sign with, but he didn't have a clue. When asked about a special girl in his life, he answered, 'I can't give her name, but there was one from afar, but it didn't work out. She still has my heart.' His words resonated in my soul; like a trumpet that called out the sun in the midst of a dark storm. I was pretty sure the girl in the article was me. The need to see Marcus became so intense; I just wanted to make up for all the distress I'd caused, congratulate him on his article and just be in his presence. I could no longer excuse the feelings I had. Our connection might not rely totally on our similar experiences, I thought. Maybe I had ignored for years a love that would have saved me from my despair with Ja'Ron.

Rushing down the stairs to get the phone, I heard a knock at the door. "Hey, baby, I just had to see you." Let down was written all over my face. It was Ja'Ron. "What's wrong? You look like you seen a ghost." After the initial shock of seeing him at the door, I came to my right mind and rushed out the door, closing it behind me. "Boy, you're trying to get me killed." He looked a little frantic and uptight and opened his coat. "Baby, I need to hide this with someone I know I can trust, at least for a hot minute." He pulled out a wad of money and put it in my pocket. "And what's that in your book bag," I asked. "A little sumthin' I need you to hide for me also," he muttered, taking it off to hand to me. Right before receiving the bag, the door opened. "Shey who is th—," Grams not finishing her sentence before intensely looking at Ja'Ron. "Young man I know you and your reputation. Who are you here to see?" He looking dumbfounded refused to answer. It was inevitable for it to come down like this. She eventually was going to find out anyway. Uuuuuuurrrrrrrrr, the rubber of an old school four door black Caprice Classic gripping the decayed pavement hit the corner and stopped in front of our door. I feared what was happening and even Ja'Ron eyes buckled. Four big dudes wearing black bulletproof jackets with The Gang Squad of the DPD written on them rushed out of the car. Ja'Ron in panic had a delayed reaction before he threw the bag and ran around the back way. Without thinking, he was trapped by a wired gate that divided our project section from the others. The Narc's scooped him up like a rag doll. "What's up with y'all, I've been with my girlfriend and her family all day. That bag ain't even mine," Ja'Ron pleaded while being handcuffed. "We finally caught you red handed," the cops voice faded as they shoved Ja'Ron in the car.

Grams repeating what Ja'Ron said, "Girlfriend," looked

at me like she wanted to take me over her knee. Thank God I was too old for that. "Sheyla, how long has this been going on?"

"It's not like that at all Grams. He was saying anything to get out of trouble."

"You take me for a fool. Girl, get out of my house before I kill you, or you kill me one!"

"Grams, Where will I go?"

Grams started throwing my belongings out the door. "I don't know, don't care, but get your stuff and get out of here," she threatened with an unsympathetic look mounted on her face. "You aren't listening to me. I barely know this guy." Her eyebrows raised up to her forehead. "And you still lying. I can't believe you." She ran up on me and grabbed my shirt, making it tight to where it was choking me. "Look! That boy is neighborhood trouble. Yo' momma did the same thing. How in Gods name are you stupid enough to follow her thoughtless ways? That boy could have had us killed and you messin' around with him. "Rather than making her more upset, possibly sparking another heart attack, I packed up my things without saying another word. I called Tasha's mom and told her about my little incident; she was more than willing to let me come stay with them. Grams had been through a lot with me, so I wasn't upset with her decision. What was upsetting was how everything went down with Ja'Ron. His actions put me in this predicament.

Ja'Ron's eyes of sorrow stared at me as the police car finally drove off after sitting in the parking lot for a good 15 minutes. I swear, empathy for him was non-existent. Seventeen years old, in addition to practically being homeless, and emotionally spent, it was all due to his selfishness. Had he not appeared and taken his drama somewhere else, I wouldn't be in this tight spot. Grams finally shut the door on me, as I waited on the sidewalk for Tash and her mother to scoop me up.

Telling Tasha about the whole incident sent her into an uproar of laughter. The fact that Ja'Ron's tough guy, mean grilling expression collapsed under strenuous duress, showed how weak he really was. "So now what are you going to do?" Tasha asked. "Um, I'm not sure I understand your question."

"You know, with all that money he tucked in your pocket before getting locked up."

That was a good question. What was I going to do? Knowing how he was, there was no way I was going to just go buck wild and spend it all. Besides, what if he beat his case and got out soon. Plus, I still felt some kind of connection and loyalty to him. No matter what he was, what he did, or how mad I was at him, he was still my first; still someone I cared deeply for.

It took a while before Grams and I spoke. My fear of how she would respond to the total truth about me and Ja'Ron kept me away, but my concern for her broke through our barriers. Every visit gave me a chance to express my love and appreciation for what she meant to me. No matter how strict she was, she really tried to protect me from self-destructing. I felt comfortable enough to hide Ja'Ron's money in her house.

Christmas day, Grams and I fellowshipped. We enjoyed one another's company that day more than any other day I could remember. The separation had done us some good. We talked about old times and my mother, and we prayed for her safe return. The Ja'Ron situation was never mentioned, which eased my comfort level, enabling me to open up.

"How is Marcus doing?"

"Grams, I haven't talked to him much these days."

"Why not? Aren't you guys still friends?"

"Well, yes, but he's been very busy and standoffish."

"Baby, can you blame him? He's been chasing you for

years, and probably needs time to get over you. Ya know, everyone has to draw the line somewhere." She picked up the gift-wrappings while she talked. It was honestly the first real conversation we had had that she talked to me, not down to me, or at me. "I'm not saying get serious. You're too young for all that, but baby, you just don't find good friends that often. And what if he is the one for the future and you let him get away?" She was keeping it real with me. It was something I'd thought about before, but her words were confirmation. "Grams, I love you. I really do." I continued to stay with Tash and her mom, but spent the weekends going to church and hanging out with my Grams. Her church was still terrible, leading me to read the Bible on my own, but the time spent with her was worth it.

Mustering up the courage to apologize and asking for Marcus forgiveness was hard to do. I let months, weeks, and days go by with Marcus and I barely speaking. Our basketball team was excelling and he was breaking all kind of school and state records. I didn't want to take a chance on messing up his flow. It was weird being a fan of someone I've known for years.

The team was closing the season undefeated. High School March Madness was getting started, and our school was on cloud nine; even coach Thomas received a lot of hype. This was it. The atmosphere was thick. Our school was on the verge of winning the state title, a feat that had avoided us for a little more than 8 years. Yes, even I, Sheyla Patron had gotten caught in the excitement.

Tasha felt like I was selling myself short by not taking advantage of my so much needed freedom. She continued to accuse me of using this new found appreciation for Marcus and basketball as a void replacement. "Tasha, Marcus is a special guy," I said in defense.

"Oh really. So why does your face look so unconvincing," Tash said rolling her eyes. My eyes went to the top of my head, trying to get assurance from my heart, but it was something I thought about often. Was I really using Marcus for my selfish ego purposes?

One day Tash asked me if I wanted to take a trip to Cancun. Her cousin Jackie wanted us to get a taste of the college atmosphere during spring break. Plus she argued it would get my head off everything, giving my swagger back. It was a no-brainer. "Yeah, but how we going to get there, and wit what money?"

"You ever count how much loot you got from Ja'Ron?"

"No, not really. After he got locked up, I hid it over Grams place around Christmas time."

"Shey, are you crazy. This is our senior year, plus Ja is locked up! With all the dirt he'd done, it done caught up wit'em. You betta enjoy yo self. He probably ain't gettin' out for a long time."

"You right. I'll use some of it, just not all of it. Yeah, we can go."

That Friday we took a plane and met Jackie down in Cancun, Mexico. She and her college roommates reserved two hotel rooms at the Oasis Paradise Hotel. The ride from the airport was about 15 minutes of admiration. Everything was so beautiful. It felt like I was in a fairytale about to click my heels together to return back to reality. Just imagine, a hood chick out and about seeing the world. A magnificent sight consumed my attention. My mouth dropped, looking at this big aquarium looking mass of space, covered in glass, reflecting my beauty in the sunlight. "Tash, don't tell me we're staying here."

"Fa sho, this is it girl," as she gave me a high five smiling.

We called Jackie and her friend's hotel room for them to meet us in the lobby. Brittany and Laura were valley girls from California. They drove down to Mexico in Laura's 1998 Explorer truck. There were masses of people, excited, and it was still afternoon. I gave Tash a high five, looked miles in front and saw a sea of people. "It's on tonight ladies," I yelled like I was cheering a football team to victory. All the pressures of what I was facing at home succumbed to the supremacy of the party milieu. Even though we were tired, there was no way we were going to let a second of this experience pass us by without participating. Thousands of college students were in the streets after the same thing; partying with no conscious. Music blasted from trunks of high powered speakers from the streets, cars, stores, you name it. There was no segregation here. Different cultures, races like blacks, whites, hispanics were just blending in like a New Orleans stew. Everyone was getting along. After walking the strip of Kukulcan Boulevard shopping, we decided to go home to change for the clubs. Tasha turned 18 years old in February, so she was good for the clubs, but little ole me hadn't reached the legal age. We tried two clubs, using fake I.D., but both were no goes. Nothing worked. The last one confiscated my fake I.D. "Hey y'all, I'm not going to spoil this evening. Go ahead and get y'all gig on. Go ahead, the hotel is right down the street. I'll walk home."

"Shey are you sure, I'll come with you," Tasha offering, but not sounding convincing.

"Girls get in there. Just tell me how it was." I must admit that did bring the rain to my parade.

Entering the hotel, I read this advertisement for a beach party that invited everyone in the hotel. Why waste an outfit that was itchin' to be seen by as many people as possible. The party had just begun and it was crunk. The pickings were plentiful. Gorgeous men were everywhere; I mean the best of the best were there. It was time to let my guard down and have fun. I stepped on the floor with two guys sandwiching me in rhythm to some calypso song. They took it too far, just a little too freaky for me. I had to step back on the sidelines and watch. Then this slow tune called 'Sunless Sky' came on. It was hot, had me wanting to put it down on the dance floor. From behind, this guy whispered in my ear, "May I have this dance?" His breath as pure as a newborn baby grabbed my awareness. His muscles grazed my right shoulder. I had to see how this guy looked. "Oh my God. What are you doing here?" I screamed jumping into his arms. It was Marcus. The coincidence of him being there put me in shock. Out of all the people, all the hotels, all the cities in the world, I see Marcus in Cancun. Without saying much he caressed me and swayed my body with his to the beat of the song. I laid my head on his chest, wrapping my arms around his body. "Marcus it is so nice to see you down here."

"Shhhh. I want you to feel this moment," he whispered, seductively kickin' game.

The song ended with a fast song following. We ignored the transition, caught in the constant rhythm of the previous slow jam, social dancing. Every feeling concerning him had surfaced. Even his cologne smelled more intense than ever, entrancing me. Marcus then led me away from the scene on down to the waterfront.

"Shey, please forgive me for giving you the cold shoulder; just trippin', holdin' grudges."

"Marcus, please don't worry about the past. Right now is all that matters."

Marcus took my hand, "Listen to the peace and calmness of the earth. Don't you wish we could have this back in Detroit?"

"Yeah, that would be nice," I said feeling like a little kid again. "Don't you have the big game this weekend, and how did you get here? Who are you with?"

"The state championship is next weekend, postponed due to some scheduling conflict that came up at Chrysler Arena. And I'm down here with Dannie and his uncle. His uncle paid our way in exchange for us selling his T-shirts."

"So why aren't you selling his shirts."

"Shey! Them shirts are wacked. Plus they got lost on the

flight, mixed up with another's flight luggage. So I'm chillin'." He said Dannie's uncle was at the club and Dannie was around the area trying to holla at any chick that was willing to give him time and space.

The sand was getting in our shoes, so we both took our shoes off and decided to walk on the edge where the trickling water barely met the sand. Marcus pointed to the stars glaring in the sky. "Just look at Gods creation. He made all of this for us to enjoy, and now I'm finally getting that chance to understand how wonderful his glory is." Everything about this moment felt so right. The fragrance that permeated from his body almost made me collapse. Unh, unh-unh snuck through my lips, hiding from his ears; my smile met both ear lobes simultaneously. Pure pleasure! A feeling that had avoided me for long time. I didn't know if it was the atmosphere that brought about these feelings and chemistry between he and I, but whatever it was, I didn't want it to end. "Marcus, I heard you had really, really gotten into church. What sparked that?" I asked.

"I don't know. It's like, no matter what dangerous situation I was in, or how painful things were, God pulled me through. You start looking at the sun, the rain, the make-up of our body, and it's no doubt that God is real. Now, the more I read the word, the more I feel his presence. You feel me."

"Marcus, it may sound strange, but I do." We then turned and just stared in each other's eyes. Srrrrrrrr, the wind slightly whistled as if it was singing the praise of this instant. Feeling me shake with a chill that ran through my body, he grabbed me closer to his warmth and held me tight. I wanted to rip his shirt off and corrupt the very innocence that at one time turned me off, now edged me on. He began to sing the song we had just slow danced to. "How can I live without you? How can I be alone? Like a Sunless Sky." His singing, a bit out off tune, but romantic in thought, was so nice. "Aaaah, that is so sweet, but don't sing again." We both burst into a big laugh. For revenge he scooped up some water and threw it on me. I chased him, tripping him with my leg; I fell on top of him. "Some big time athlete. You couldn't get away from little ole' me," I uttered softly. While laying on him, we went into a gaze again. Spluush, cruuush, the waves crashing into the nearby rocks set the tone. It took everything for me not to kiss him. "Lets go up to my room," Marcus insisted. I didn't know what was next, but I trusted him with every inch of my conscious indwelling.

He led me to his room's outside balcony, showcasing the ocean. The wind at a calm breeze put us in a relaxed state. He gently caressed my shoulders as we laid side by side on the cot. Marcus then turned to face me, grazing my lips with his by mistake, sparking us to engage in a soft kiss. His tongue barely touching mine ended briefly and innocently. We began to talk and talk all through the night until we fell asleep. I woke up right before sunrise, knowing Tash was probably worried. Just hovering over his sleeping body, him looking so peaceful and giving me such a romantic night put a smile on my face that was imprinted permanently.

The Decision!
MARCUS......

Colleges, Colleges, Colleges were hounding me. I received a letter from every school in the country. My grandmother refused to sway me in any direction. "Boy, this is your life, and grandma only wants what's best for you. You have to decide as a young man." All the schools were promising, but I was kind of leaning towards the University of North Carolina. The history and tradition of the likes of Michael Jordan, James Worthy, Jerry Stackhouse, Rasheed Wallace to name a few attracted me a whole lot. The madness increased when we found out the NBA now was interested. Experts placed me in the late first round if I declared myself eligible for the NBA draft. It was quite tempting, had I been predicted to go early in the first round, I would've entered the draft without a doubt. Between choosing what was next in my future, my girlfriend, or the lack there of, the upcoming state championship, and my mom's murderer; I was becoming increasingly tired of the everyday hustle and bustle. The headache's started reoccurring, which was always a sign that I mentally had to let something go. Stress confronted me with a vengeance.

"Son, I would like to see you for a second," coach called me into his office.

"Yes, Coach. What's going on?"

"Well, let's just say you might be talking to the next head coach at the University of Detroit," coach spoke with an excitement like he won the lottery.

"That's tight. This is what you've been wanting."

"I should know in a few weeks. Don't tell anyone, just in case I don't get the job."

The news was very exciting. It now gave Dannie a better chance at getting a scholarship to hoop. "Coach, what do you suggest regarding the NBA versus college."

"Well, Marcus, you have all the ability in the world, but you're not ready for the NBA. It's made for mature men. If you're projected in the first round, but fall to the second, you just may disappear. Develop your game in college then talk about the NBA. Rather it's only for a year or two, just prepare before making that step. If you're worried about injury, a potential NBA prospect could have insurance taken out for millions of dollars through the NCAA to protect himself financially. So those are just a few things to contemplate," coach teaching his usual life decisions 101.

"Well what College should I attend coach."

"That's up to you. Which provides basketball opportunities, a great education, and a place where you would be comfortable is the school for you. That's a decision only Marcus Stunson can make."

I was picked to play in the McDonalds All-American game. Coach and I also discussed the itinerary that was sent to him for this game that's televised on national television. Things were whining down in my senior year. We were undefeated, heading to the state finals. Out of all the top players in the country, I was the only one to average a triple double for the season–35 points, 10 rebounds, and 11 assist. While in the office talking, a basketball coach from some university called to see if I would take a visit to their school. Coach declined for me, knowing I'd already cut down my choices to four schools.

After leaving his office, I met Sheyla coming around the corner. "Hey Marcus, and how are you?"

"Oh what up. I'm all good. Gotta catch you later, got practice. The big game is coming up. Holla." It hurt me to cold shoulder her, but my choices were limited. Either be friends and continue to get my heart crushed, or move on.

A few days before the championship game we got news that the game had to be rescheduled. I was upset. "Stun, chillout. I got something we can do. It'll get yo head out the clouds, no whatum sayin', dawg."

And what's that," I asked.

"My uncle just started this new line of clothes and he needs people to help promote his shirts in Cancun, Mexico during the college spring break. He'll pay our way if we help him."

It sounded like a plan to me. After having Dannie's uncle talk to my grandmother, we were good to go.

I never heard much about Spring Break, but listening to Dannie tell me what we were about to encounter, I was wound up. It was later in the day when we arrived. Dannie's Uncle Paul was just a cussin' because his luggage, carrying his shirts was on the wrong flight. Every time he opened his mouth, a cuss' word came out. He was a funny character. After checkin' into our room, we decided to hang out. Uncle Paul still upset said he was leaving us to drink his pain away. Dannie and I decided to go to the party that the hotel set up for their guest on the beach. "Dawg, women in bikinis. You can't beat that," Dannie screaming, pullin' his hat over his eyes. Just to think, two characters in the same family.

On the dance floor from a distance it looked like I saw Sheyla dancing with two guys. It was impossible for this to

Retraced

be. I asked Dannie if that was her and he didn't have a clue. "Yo, while you go check that out. I'll be on the prowl. Don't expect me to report in anytime soon."

By the time I made it to the dance floor. The young lady stopped dancing. After realizing it was Shey, I decided to surprise her. It sparked a time in my life that I'll never forget. We held each other and talked like we hadn't seen each other in years. Destiny revealed itself, authenticating my belief that we were meant to be. How else could you explain the night we had. It ended with me kissing her. Her lips were so soft. Goosebumps covered my entire body. I grabbed her closer and slowly kissed her again just to prove to myself that I wasn't dreaming.

On the flight back, I told Dannie what happened. Instead of congratulating me, he went out on me. "You's a fool. Look at the set up. Stun is all of sudden on magazines, groupies hounding him, NBA scouts coming to high school basketball games. I don't know if you know, but ole' girl's boyfriend got locked up. Dawg, it's easy to like you now. She ain't nuthin' but a opportunist. I'm yo boy, I ain't gon' lie to you. Think, just think, and quit reacting with yo emotions." Dannie was animated with every word. How could I ignore his point? He made sense.

"This is what I've been askin' for."

"Stun, is it the challenge of you finally getting her, 'cause nobody can be that much in love wit' anyone?"

"I'm sho it's love. I really love the girl," I said lowering my tone of voice.

"No it ain't is it? Let me see. Big Stun, the star basketball player can't take losin'. He never fails at anything."

"That's far from the truth. I have fail! Everything that was meaningful I fell short at." I said while noticing we were getting the other passenger's attention.

"Like what Stun! Like what have you ever failed!" Dannie said in an aggressive whisper.

My emotions were stirred. Tears were on the brink, I tried to hold back my emotions but couldn't, ignoring all the people watching. "I failed my mother! Man I was right there, you understand. Maybe if I had screamed, let the punk know I was there, she might still be here. I failed and now she's dead. She's dead D'." The words oozed out giving me some relief. Dannie was at a lost for words. He just looked at me. "D,' man, being with her takes my mind away from that incident. When I'm in her presence, nothin' else matters. Before her, basketball was the only thing that did that for me." The plane ride had gotten a little heated and I noticed everyone looking at us; I had to break the tension. After wiping my tears and clearing my voice I asked, "Well D, what did you get into?"

"Let's just say if any girl from Cancun claim she's pregnant by me, you know nuthin'," Dannie laughing as he spoke, trying to lighten the mood. All I could do was nod my head; he was as crazy as ever because he probably was tellin' the truth.

When we touched ground, we knew we were back in Detroit. No more shorts, hello jackets and coats. My grandmother greeted me by telling me Ms. Priscilla called from Flint. I called her immediately. We hadn't talked in two years. Hearing her voice was so refreshing. "I'm so proud of you. I've been keeping updates on you. Keep it up boy," Ms. Priscilla spoke encouraging words. She promised to attend my championship game.

During the week of school, it was evident my relationship with Shey changed. She went out of her way to walk me to every class. Even though my talk with Dannie haunted my thoughts, I was able to ignore our conversation. Shey was coming to school looking so fly. She took it to another level by having blonde highlights in her hair, giving a more mature, sexy look. Anyways, the time had come for us to play for the state championship. Right before the game, Coach announced to the team that he was accepting the University of Detroit's head coaching position. My teammates screamed in unison, "lets win this one for coach." Before getting on the bus heading to Chrysler Arena, I stopped to pick up my gym shoes out of my locker. When I opened the door, a big balloon attached to a note jumped out at me.

"Will you go with me, and be my boyfriend? Circle yes or no!'
Sheyla Patron

The biggest grin in history appeared on my blushing face. I went to the game on a mission. The game began with me setting the tone. Off the back I stole the ball on a break away, completing a double clutch backwards dunk. The crowd roared in hysterics, cheering us on to an 85 to 70 victory. Sheyla caught in the stampede of our celebrating peers couldn't find her way to me. I charged bypassing everyone that ran up to me to greet her in the middle of the floor. " Shey, yes. The answer is yes." Shey embraced my neck giving me a sweet kiss on the lips. "I had to let them screaming girls jockin' you know that you are taken," she whispered in my ear. Finally there was someone greeting me with love at the end of our game; everything fit so well. I knew then what school I was going to attend. I set up a news conference for that Monday to announce my basketball future.

With all the news cameras, students, and teachers gathered in the gym watching my every move, I forgot what I was supposed to say. Coach was waving his hands back and forth, trying to get me to speak. He continued gesturing. It didn't spark my memory, so he started pointing down and I read his lips. "Read the paper." I looked down, remembering my speech was already written. "Iah…I.. I..hope this doesn't come as a disappointment for some, and doesn't shock all the coaches and schools that wanted me to sign with them." I paused to take a deep breath. "I've decided to ignore the NBA's seductive invite and take my skills to the University of Detroit. Hopefully they'll accept me. That's right, I'm staying home." It was a good minute before anyone responded. Mouths all across the gym dropped. Then I heard sporadic claps consecutively. Coach ran up to me, "Marcus are you sure? Don't come because of me."

"Coach, a lot of things played a part in this decision. This is where I want to be. You and I will lead that little school to basketball supremacy."

Dannie rushed over and grabbed me. "Stun, what in the world are you doing? All of these big schools that play on national TV every week wanting you, and you chose U of D. You're letting Sheyla decide yo future."

"D, chill out. She didn't even know about the decision. I'll put the school on the map," I boastfully stated my claim. Right after the announcement, it was announced I had won the Mr. Basketball award. I was the first Mr. Basketball player in the school's history to sign with U of D.

The Will of Right vs. Wrong

Shey and I talked every night. Both of our grandparents were so happy that we were dating. It was never an issue with us visiting each other. I wanted to spend every second with her, but there were a lot of demands on my time. With the different high school All-Star basketball events I was involved in, we mostly saw each other during school hours. Church also became our main meeting ground. She decided that she wanted to become a member of my church. My fear was that she was only doing it for me. Shey swore up and down her relationship with the Lord had everything to do with her desire to serve Christ, so how could I question that.

One weekend I had free, Shey took me out in a car she had bought. It was old, but it ran. "Hey, how did you get the money to pay for this car?"

"Well, before Ja'Ron got locked up, he gave me some money," Shey looked me in the eyes to see my reaction.

"Have you heard from that cat?"

"No Marcus. "

"So when are you going to let him know you and I are together."

"I'll write him. It's not really none of his business anyways. But to make you feel good, I'll do it."

"Shey you still feel for that guy don't you?"

"Where is that comin' from? I'm over him," Sheyla protested.

"And what did your grandmother say about the car?"

"She thinks Tash's moms got it for me."

"Yeah right. Even if that was true, why are you lying to her? You know the Lord doesn't like that. Plus what's done in the dark, eventually comes to the light."

"Marcus do not put religion in my face. I'm trying now, please chill out."

This night was the first argument we had. She ended up laughing, telling me that she was happy with me and me only. We drove to the drive-in to watch 'Love Can't Wait'. The beginning of the movie was impossible to describe to anyone had anyone asked. Watching the screen, Shey began to peck my neck delicately with her succulent lips. It sparked our first real passionate kiss. I then returned the favor and kissed her neck. She moaned my name, "Oh Marcus." The strength that repressed the growing sexual tension had lost its stamina, fighting without a defense, on the verge of giving in. Treasuring celibacy until marriage, I was embarrassed thinking she would be turned off, so I didn't say anything; just played it off by telling her my back was aching; bringing our actions to a halt. "Could you give me a massage Shey?" Awkwardness set in, causing us to leave before the movie ended. "Marcus, I wish my mom was here to see who God put in my life. I can't believe I feel this way about you," Sheyla belted out of her gut, almost dropping a tear.

"You have no idea how that makes a brotha feel. I've loved you from the first time we hung out in my grandmother's basement."

"That's cute. You still remember that," she said while rubbing her fingers through her hair, looking so sexy.

"Have you heard from yo moms recently?"

"Not in a minute. She's still runnin' and hiding like she's a criminal with her no good boyfriend. Oooh, I hate that Terry," Shey spoke under her breath to hide her frustration.

"Yeah, I feel you. The Terry I know, I hate to. Sorry Lord. But that cat, I'd kill if I had a chance," I said meaning it, but not literally.

"Hey at least we know not to name our kids Terry," Shey laughed pinching my cheeks.

SHEYLA......

Tasha teased me about being with Marcus. It was hard convincing her that my feelings for him were genuine. He treated me like a princess, a feeling that people only dream about. She was clownin' me anyways, because I started getting more involved in church. Refusing to do a lot of things I once did, she avoided me sometimes. Plus, the little time that was allotted with Marcus's schedule, I tried to spend that with him, so Tash wasn't feeling the whole set up. Especially being I stayed with her. "Are you going to at least go shopping with me," Tash asked, walking away as if she knew my answer was no."

"You know I want to, but Marcus is having the big press conference today. Let's hook up later." She took off without responding.

The news conference was held in our school's gym. No words could describe the joy I felt when Marcus announced he was going to stay home and attend school here in the city. You can say I pretty much had a long distance relationship with Ja'Ron, so I already experienced how separation could kill a relationship. Marcus became one of the most recognizable faces in Michigan. It was mad write-ups about him being such a big basketball name attending such a small school. Some fans appreciated his ability to resist the glitz and glam, but some people called him a coward, scared to perform in the spotlight. Nothing bothered him. Between his humility and his faithfulness to God, he inspired me to become a better Christian and a better person. Not getting so caught up in self, but honoring and loving others. My mom was still living, Grams survived a heart attack, Ja'Ron is out of my life, and he gave me a God-fearing boyfriend. God had been so good to me. We didn't have the kind of time to spend with each other, but every minute counted. One day he played in this All-Star basketball game that was televised nationally. I told everyone I knew that my boyfriend was playing on TV. One thing that didn't change with me was the fact that I still loved attention. Tasha's mom was loving it, because she knew Marcus too. My girl Tash was hatin', acting like she didn't care that Marcus was on TV. When Marcus came home and finally had a weekend to spend with me. The day before our long awaited date, I purchased a 1992 Taurus from a used car lot. Ja'ron gave me a total of $7,000, and I spent $3,000 of that on the Cancun trip and the car.

One day Ja'Ron called me. Tasha's mom picked up the phone, with her face turning from a smile to an instant frown. "Shey, this is a collect call from the county building. You know these calls are expensive. Tell whoever that fool is that no more calls will be accepted here. That goes for you and Tash," Tasha's mom spoke with in irritated tone.

"What's up with my girl? Sorry about not trying to get in touch with you sooner, but I had to hit up some folks that could pay this $500,000 bail."

"No problem, I figured you had to get your stuff in order" nervously trying to figure out how to tell him I was through with him, and dating Marcus.

"It's been a few months, so what's been up witchu? Did

you get a chance to put that loot up?"

"Not much has been up, but did you get enough money for your bail?" Trying to divert his attention away from his questions.

"Not yet. I got a hook up out of town though. Just hadn't been able to get up with the guy. But you didn't answer my question."

"I ah, I spent some of it to go on a small trip with Tasha. Wait, there's more. I ah, well, ah, I purchased a car too."

"How much did you spend," Ja'Ron responded shockingly calm.

"$3,000"

"Heeey, do not spend another dime. But on the real, I expected you to spend some of it. Don't worry about it, I thought you at first was going to say you were breaking up wit a brotha."

Flushed in guilt, my initial approach to just bluntly tell him had to be altered, trying to elusively avoid his wrath. "Ja, I didn't think you wanted to be with me any longer. Before you got locked up, your attention wasn't me. What I'm trying to say is, after not hearing from you even when you got locked up, I figured it was time for me to move on. And that's kinda what I did."

"Who is it Shey? Don't tell me Stun," Ja'Ron spoke transitioning from his calm voice to the frustrated.

Before speaking, I pondered on rather it was the best thing to do. To tell him the truth could mean him straight trippin', and who needed that drama in their live, but I was left without choices. "Marcus and I have gotten closer," I uttered in relief, just to get it over, ready to deal with the consequences if need be.

"Oh this is how you gon' do me, right. Wait until I get out! He ended his paroxysm by slamming the phone in my ear.

The Prom

After a few close calls, Marcus and I promised to do my best to allow ourselves to be in positions that would invoke that possibility of me devirginizing him. Sex was never a big part of my life, but once you've had it, and to now be with out was something I never expected. Celibacy became an enemy, hard for me to live up to. I commended his ability to stay true to his commitment. It really encouraged me to fight for celibacy.

Our relationship grew into a force of love to where I hated being out of his sight. In class, my mind was often preoccupied with Marcus's smile, his laughter, his patience made him stand out from everyone. We even shopped together on the days he had off from profiling his celebrity. Shopping for the right outfit for the prom was out cold and challenging. Our financial resources were limited. It was hard getting use to not having the funds to just purchase the clothes I really wanted. Fighting to stay out of the rest of Ja'Ron's stash had me on edge. I swore the money talked to me, "Buy your clothes with me. Buy your dress with me." Our dates had to incur a lot of creativity to make up the difference of not having money. Most times we just ended up over his house watching old TV flicks. Marcus had all kind of people willing to buy and give him things, but he was so paranoid over NCAA violations, possibly hurting his basketball eligibility for the upcoming year, that he rejected everything. If there was anything haunting me about the break up with Ja'Ron, it was the money and physical withdrawal of getting my groove on. "What I can't do for you now, I'll make up the difference when I make it to the league," Marcus repeated often in defense of competing with my apparent need for the finer things in life.

My birthday was the day before prom. Understanding that Marcus didn't have much money, I wasn't anticipating anything but his attention. Besides, if it came down to it, I'd gotten comfortable with claiming Ja'Ron's money as mine. I was planning on just dipping in the candy jar just one more small time. It was by coincidence that this was the same day I received mail from Ja'Ron.

Hey baby,

I don't have a lot to say, but I been thinkin' that you deserve someone on your team. Please forgive me. I'm not mad at you, just askin' for a fair chance once I get out of this hellhole. The months that I been up in here, I now know what kind of a women you was. It's hard to think that that girl is now wit sum sucka from around the way. Talkin' to my lawya', it looks like I can get out soon. I'll be seeing you baby.

Luv 4life!

PS- Don't worry about the cash you spent.

Just give the rest to my mutha please!!!!!!
Ja'Ron

Reading his letter brought about mixed emotions. How prepared was I to seeing him again. We've shared deep intimate moments, so we were connected emotionally. Agony set in bringing my relationship with Marcus to the forefront. I was scared to mess up what he and I had established. "Happy birthday boo," Marcus gaping in my eyes as he entered my bedroom.

"Hey sweety, thank you."

"What's that you're reading," he asked.

"Oh nothing, an old letter, that's all," I nervously whispered, hoping he wouldn't ask to read it.

"Everyone is downstairs waiting for the star of the show. Hurry up slow poke," he said exiting my room.

The gifts I received were very special, but the one that stood out most was the gifts Marcus gave me. He made a coupon book of love. Each page had something different. My favorite was the slave coupon. Where he was my slave to do anything I asked for a few hours on any given Saturday. Of course it had exceptions of anything morally questionable, but that was known without being stated. He was so sweet. Then he gave me his McDonalds All-American jump suit. The jogging suit the team wore on a promotional visit to see cancer patients. It had all the signatures of his teammates. "Shey this sweat shirt has the top players in the country on it. It should be worth some money in a few years when some of us make it to the show," Marcus said referring to the NBA. His gift surpassed anything I had ever received. He gave something that was dear to him. My heart couldn't wait to spend Prom night with him.

Prom day had come. I decided to go to the Encore Hair Salon to let one of Detroit Metro's best hairstylist, they call Paula the duchess of hair; hook me up. This was where

Tasha's mom went, which usually was out of my price range, but for this occasion, it was well worth it. I had to look like a million dollars. My hair was whipped, receiving all kind of compliments; the night was ready to receive its queen. Marcus along with two of his teammates and their dates parked, scooping me up from my Grams house in a stretch black limousine. Dressed in a black tux hanging perfectly off his limbs had my baby looking like a prince. He had a white on white tie, vest and shirt combination that had the girls in my complex staring in awe. My boo looked good. "Look at my baby," Grams looking on with emotional tears falling from her eyes, trying to take snapshots of us. She was so happy to see I had finally given in to Marcus advances. "Y'all have a good time, be safe."

The night progressed with us just bonding. His teammates were cool. These were the same people I had ignored and dogged out for a while, yet they were very receiving of me and Marcus being together. My girl Tash was early for once with some grown dude looking older than our parent and teacher chaperones. They were dancing on the dance floor like they were the only couple dancing. She was just a-swinging her big ole hips everywhere. Sweating, huffing and puffing, it was hilarious. You could tell the chaperones were a little reluctant to ask them to chill out with the dirty dancing. For God sakes, her date was one of their peers. Our little entourage sat back and enjoyed the show. They were clownin'.

While sitting down, Ree Ree came over. "Shey would you mind if Marcus and I have a dance?" Either I had boo boo the fool written on my face, or she was just crazy enough to get smacked in hers. "Uh, what do I look like? Go take your trifling self right back over to who ever you came here wit," I uttered trying to control my temper, not allowing the project girl in me out.

"Shey, I came over here politely, not to start trouble.

This is our last year together, and I just wanted to have, I guess you can say a last dance with Marcus Stunson. Now is that alright with you Marcus?"

"Tramp did you or didn't you get my point," I screamed and stood up in her face about to let my fist go.

Marcus immediately stood up with an expression as if he was enjoying the little catfight we were about to engage in. "Lady's hold on. Ree, thank you, but I'm here with my girl. Shey chill out and give me a hug," he said holding back his laugh.

Ree turned with an attitude back towards her table swingin' her hips. "You betta take yo triflin' a—," I didn't finish the sentence, interrupted by Marcus, "Shey don't even go there."

"What. No What! I wasn't going to say nuthin' but trifling applehead," I continued with a smirk on my face.

"Yeah right."

I couldn't believe I had gotten so mad. I never go to the profane to express myself, but I just felt so disrespected. And then that song came on calming my nerves; Sunless Sky. "Marcus this is our song. Remember in Cancun."

"Yeah I know," he responded taking my hand. We danced and grooved on the small piece of floor left by Tasha, Ree Ree and their dates. He loosened the button that held his bowtie together, showing his hair lying on his chest. The fragrance on his neck was unveiled as it made me caress his back. The disco light reflected on his skin, which showed a dimple in his cheek every time he smiled. My baby was lookin' good. He wrapped his arms around my waste, leading me side to side with each beat that kept the song on pace. My heart fluttered. A tingling sensation infiltrated my body. The closer he grabbed me to his body, the more I tingled; sending shivers throughout my body. Lord knows I wanted to have that boy right then and there. When the song came to an end, Marcus kissed me very long and intimately. It was a kiss that made my toes quiver; I was on the verge of busting out of my big-heeled Cinderella shoes. Our kiss was unlike any other, in fact it took a chaperone to come and tap us on our shoulders, letting us know we were getting too carried away. "Sorry," Marcus whispered looking so embarrassed.

When the Prom ended, we decided to leave with Tasha and her date. They had a hotel room in the Renaissance Center and invited more of our schoolmates. It was plush. Entering the room, Marcus looked weirded out. The drinks and rowdiness the crowd exuded was too much for him. We decided to excuse ourselves and went into a separate room away from everyone.

After stepping in the room we closed the door. I took his hand, "I'm really enjoying myself tonight. Thank you for pursuing me for all those years."

"Thank you for finally given in. Right now means so much to me," he expressed running his hand through my hair. It was too much for me. I just laid him down, lying directly on top of him; slithering my body on his to stimulate a moment I wanted badly. The heat of the moment cornered him in submission. He caressed me, while we kissed. Right after I thought I had him, he slid from under me. "Shey, please don't be mad, but I can't. I'm really committed to my walk with Christ. I love you, but I love the Lord more. Do you understand?"

Like a flash of lightning my soul was instantly convicted and I begged, "Please, please, please don't think less of me. I really respect your strength and your walk. I even pray I can have that kind of strength one day. Lord forgive me. Marcus you forgive me to."

"Come on girl. That moment with you, I wish will come sooner than you think. But I only want it in marriage," he stated while putting both his hands on top of his head. He later called Dannie asking him to pick us up.

MARCUS......

Shey and Stun, written on my heart for life. It was an unbelievable feeling having a dream come to pass. The girl of my dreams had finally gotten on board on the journey of love with me as guide. The Prom was here, and Shey was my date. Ree Ree saw me prior to the prom, trying to entice me with her usual seductive walk. "Marcus I know you and Shey are kickin' it, but you know you really a need a true date. Someone you can really have fun with."

"Let me guest who that person might be. You," I answered.

"Yeah me. Who else," she responded tilting her head, letting her weave hang over her ear."

"Ree you got a boyfriend. Plus I couldn't do that to Shey. But thanks for the invite," I rushed off to end our conversation.

Some of my teammates and I decided to go in on a stretch limousine. I was the first picked up for the Prom. It was the night I anticipated, the night that memories are engraved in high school student's minds forever. Gathering the fellas and their dates, it was now time to pick up Shey. Shocked into a gaze looking at how her makeup was gently placed on her caramel complexion made me gasp for air. She was dressed in a cream dress caressing every curve that exemplified womanhood, creating an audience of awe with all eyes following her every whim and gesture. Shey out did herself, having a rust like shawl cover her shoulders added the finishing touch to her overall splendor. "Shey, you are so beautiful. My eyes have been blessed by your company," I uttered while ignoring everything around me.

My homie Dannie took some girl that he asked at the last minute. He stared at Sheyla's girl Tasha all night. Apparently he still was a little fond of Tash and her ghetto-ism. The prom was pretty cool though. The room was covered in blue and gold balloons. We were seated at our tables, placed on the tables were plastic wine glasses, with apple cider drinks in the middle of the table. It wasn't as hype as I expected, but memorable. I couldn't believe that Ree Ree asked to dance with me with Shey sitting there. Then Shey was about to act a fool, all over me. It was crazy, but when we got on the dance floor and kissed, I felt a touch of heaven dissipating anything that was there to spoil the mood. By the end of the night we were tempted, but I was able to remain strong for the both of us.

Love in the Midst of War

It had all come down to our graduation. I noticed Shey was kind of down. Knowing she hated high school, it was my conclusion that it couldn't have been that. Graduating and her mom not there to support her was my assessment. I didn't want to bring it up, but if she found fit to discuss it with me, my ears were available. "Marcus, how do you handle not having your mom around, especially for events like this one," Shey asked with a frown defining her mood.

"It hurts. I would guess it's different for you. My mom will never be there for me, but in yo' case you know your mom is livin' and have the capability to see you if she tried. It's hard to answer that one Shey."

"Yeah I know. But it hurts. She's just so scared of T.C. Man I hate him so much."

"T.C. Shey are you referring to Terry, the man your mom ran off with," I asked trying to get clarity.

"Yes Marcus"

"Is his full name Terry Clemons?"

"Yeah! Oh you heard about him too on the news."

"Shey, that's the cat that killed my mom. Terry Clemons! All these years and yo mom was hiding out with this cat. The man that killed my mother! I'm dating the stepdaughter of my mom's killer!"

"How do you know it's just not a coincidence? I mean Terry Clemons is a common name," she stood up to defend against my accusation.

"Think about it. A Terry Clemons, nicknamed T.C., and a murderer. It ain't that kinda coincidence existing nowhere in the world. This is the same guy. I betchu that was him in Ohio. I'm going to find'em. Just watch!"

"Baby and do what. Just chill out and tell the police."

"Look, have the police found out where your mom is? NO! Did they listen to me the first time I told them about the killer? NO! Didn't you tell me that they ran a trace on a phone call you received from your mom? What became of it? Nothing! Can't you see they don't care? I'm straight on them; I'll handle it myself." My graduation day had turned into a memory of despair. The day I found out I was dating the stepdaughter of my mother's killer. The ceremony went by with me barely remembering anything. My heart was focused on ending the pain that had been haunting me for years–the murder of my beloved mother.

THE SUMMER HEAT

The heat from the summer shimmer was torching my skin. It was hot as can be mixed in with emotion that was hot for revenge. My love for Shey was even being challenged by my hate for Terry Clemons. So I gave us some distance just to clear my head. During this time Dannie and I was able to register for school. We were set up to room together at The University of Detroit. Coach arranged for Dannie to go to school on a partial basketball scholarship. We hung out mostly everyday during the summer. "Dannie will you take me up to Ohio."

"For what?" He asked.

"I need to see if that cat I saw in Ohio really is Terry Clemons."

"Man I always knew you were crazy. What could you do? You ain't gotta gun, no back up, and you know I ain't 'bout to get a mark on this pretty face."

"How 'bout you let me borrow your car," I begged.

"I ain't letting you go up there by yo'self."

We took the three-hour trip to Cleveland, finding a hotel that sat right behind the McDonalds I thought to have seen T.C. at. I swear we walked up and down every street surrounding the area. We stopped in and out of the Mickey D's, no sign of him. Then I decided to ask people around the area had they heard of a guy named Terrence, T.C. After four hours passed, Dannie snapped. "Stun, do you really think my mans would be stupid enough to use his real name? You dumber than you look."

"Are you going to help or complain," I replied, knowing he was right.

We left with me in frustration. I really had no idea of what I wanted to do, besides swingin' on the chump. My heart was filled with hate. Had I had a gun, I'm for sure I would have used it. It was time to check myself. I was trying to be a man of God, but the fight to live right ain't an easy one, and I was failing. The justice never given to my mom had to be resolved. That was the only way for peace to abide in me.

HEART BREAK SHEYLA......

Graduation should have been an exciting time in my life, but it wasn't. Where was my mother? This was the time to have her see her little girl walk across the stage; something neither she nor my Grams did. High school wasn't the best experience, but it was a lot of security in being a teenager. I was ending one stage in my life, and had no clue on what was my next step. Marcus had his life all planned out, and here I am, no motivation to do anything outside of chillin'. Why hadn't I made any plans? Why didn't Grams force me to make them? After thinking, it was clear that I never allowed her the chance to help me in those areas. Grown old me thought I knew everything. So I needed comforting, leading me to ask Marcus a question that led up to a confrontation that I refused to accept as truth. How foul would it be for my mother to really be with the same guy who murdered my boyfriend's mother?

Ever since that little confrontation with Marcus, It seemed as if he looked at me differently. He still came around, but not as often, and his eyes were missing that glow. I could tell that this T.C. thing was still eating at him.

When he told me he was going to go to Ohio to look for Terry, I was very afraid for him, but what could I do. He was a man now, and maybe this was the only way to bring back the Marcus Stunson I began to deeply care for. When he came back from his Ohio trip, I was so happy to see him. But his soul was still missing. "Marcus please let me help you," I pleaded.

"Shey it's not you. I'm really okay, so don't worry alright."

His words weren't comforting. I knew he was trying to hide his pain. The only thing that got to him during heavy times was basketball.

I was so happy that the college basketball season was approaching. I knew this was when he was most relaxed. After practice, I would catch him jogging around his entire dormitory. He was a hard worker and dedicated to entering next year's NBA draft. This was when I started seeing the man I adored return to his old self. To talk to him and get anything out of the conversation, I swear basketball had to be mentioned. "Shey this is my only and last year in college," was said so much to where he should have wrote a song about it. His intense drive even pushed me. I'd been working part-time at this local grocery store. Working at the store wasn't by choice. I had no funding for college and the good jobs rejected me. Grams let it be known that I was going to work, go to school, or get out. Me, out of all people working at the freaking grocery store. It was a far cry from being headed in the right direction. "Shey, you should focus on something you like doing. I know for a fact packing groceries isn't one of them," Marcus exhausted from working out barely getting the words out.

"You're right. Well I do like doing hair."

"Enroll in some type of hair school then."

"That's it. I'll do that. Get a loan and just strive to get my license to do hair." I stepped closer to him to give him a hug. "Yeah. When I get to the league I'll help you even start yo' own chain of Salons," Marcus smiled giving me a hug while escorting me up to his dorm room.

Walking on campus felt like I was in stride with the King of England. There were always stares from fans and people admiring Marcus's star quality. Before his first game, the news reporters were constantly following him around, asking repetitive questions. They began to even ask questions concerning me. It bothered him a little, but I couldn't lie; the attention was straight to me. My schedule at the grocery market fluctuated a lot. Marcus was having his first game, which was really a scrimmage against a pro-am team. My intent was to make the game, but with Michigan's typical fall weather, being cold and rainy, I missed the entire game. I decided to surprise Marcus and meet him at his dorm room.

While parking my car in the visitor's area I saw my girl's car. Tasha was visiting. I figured she was trying to hook up with me. That was good, because after graduation, I moved back with Grams, and she moved out on her own. We talked a lot, but didn't get a chance to see each other; compliments to my job, and the late nights she worked showcasing at local strip clubs. Approaching Marcus's dorm room, I heard strange whimpering noises, sounding like someone was in trouble. Their door was cracked so I slowly pushed the door open to make sure everything was okay. I couldn't believe what was happening before my eyes. Tasha was moaning while half under the covers with Marcus face buried in between her breast, not revealing his deceiving eyes. My soul was in disarray, to the point to where the world should have shook with my emotions. My eyes filled with tears, ran wild and out of control. "How could this be, my best friend and Marcus out of all people," I thought. No wonder he wouldn't allow me to be with him. He had my slutty friend handling his needs. As I rushed out the room in panic, barely making it down the stairs, I could hear Tasha rush to close the door yelling, "whoever you are, don't come back you perverted peepin' Tom." Running in the freezing rain, I couldn't catch my breath. So I sat at the nearby bench crying my heart out. "I should go up there and beat her down," I yelled, trying to calm down. The pain of this being my best friend for years, and he my boyfriend. She was talking about how he was a busta, or how I didn't need to be with him; now she was doing him. Devastation wasn't the word. I felt like death. "God why are you allowing all of this to happen to me! I can't take it!"

SHE TRIPPIN MARCUS......

The basketball court was the world that allowed me to rule it, also to relax. During tough times, basketball was simply my sanctuary. Everyday after practice, around 6:30pm I would run a couple of times around our dorms to build my strength and stamina. Picking this small school, many eyes were going to be on me to see if my decision was the best. My goal was to take this school to the NCAA tournament and to set myself up to be drafted early in the first round of the NBA draft. My relationship with Shey was getting better. She would visit me from time to time after I practiced and ran my laps. She helped me deal with the press and all the fans that wouldn't leave me alone. Everyone was anxious to see how I lived up to playing for this small school. My decision to play for U of D was unheard of, so I had developed a lot of naysayers that said I would get lost in the crowd and become the forgotten. These pessimistic people really didn't know what kind of man they were dealing with. I had so much to prove and my goal of getting away from poverty was so strong that I wasn't willing to let anything hinder my aspirations. Our first game

Retraced

was really a scrimmage, playing against former collegiate and NBA players who were trying to re-establish their past success.

The game ended with me scoring 40 points, which sent the news reporters on a hounding mission. I refused to answer any questions, a little disturbed that my girl was nowhere insight. After the game I decided to run off some steam and just to keep pace with a habit that I knew would serve me right in the end. After getting a last minute run in, I was tired and weary. I walked in on Dannie and Tasha rushing to put on their clothes. You're talking shocked, I couldn't believe these two. All these years of ignoring each other, now they were creeping. "Tash, what's going on witcha? Looks like you were having a lot of fun tonight," I laughed turning the other way while she continued to dress.

"Boy shut up! Just worry about you and Shey, and leave me alone" Tasha sounding irritated. She walked out the door in a hurry.

"Dannie, what was up with that?"

"Dawg, she came to the game, and right after that we rushed over here. After talking, and me telling her that I thought she was the bomb, one thing led to another. I'm just glad you ain't comin' preachin' like you usually do."

"Yo, do I sense a bit of conviction going on. Man, Shey would never believe what just happened. Not to get off the subject, but yo did you peep out Ms. Priscilla at the game? D, we kicked it for a minute, but she was all over coach. Ever since I introduced them at the state finals, he said they've kept in touch. Coach, and now you, I feel kinda like cupid," I nodded my head, approving the fact that I was the man.

A few days passed without hearing from Sheyla. I was very worried, so I decided to visit her at work. Trying to talk to her was trying to ask Janet Jackson personal questions while performing on stage. Confusion wasn't the word. I began thinking the girl was crazy. What had I done this time? After embarrassing myself by following her around the grocery market for a good 20 minutes, I finally gave up. This time I was heated. She was trippin' without rhyme or reason. After a few more calls to her house, a week went by; still no response. My anger was released on the court where I had broken a U of D freshmen single game record, scoring 62 points against Iowa Tech University. The media went berserk after I followed that game up with a 35 point, 13-assist performance. My mission had begun. I was positioning myself to be drafted pretty high.

The following day I woke up starving, so I borrowed Dannie's car to go get Mickey D's. I know I was still in Detroit, but it was Déjà vu. Out of the corner of my eye, this big gruffy looking dude, frowning, had walked outside. I followed, because I knew, I just knew. That same feeling was there, the one where fear and revenge merged. My passion boiling inside beat out rationalization, it was on.

"Terry," I called out to see his response. The man flinching trying to hold back his response indicated to me that this indeed was him. The right hand left my side, connecting right on his jaw. He fell against his car. "Not so tough now are you?" I rushed him, not giving him a chance to go into his pockets, or retaliate with a punch. With his powerful arms, he swung me off, and then threw a punch. He missed, and I countered with an upper cut. "Uuuh," he gasped. I was distracted as a lady screamed and ran out of his car. "Baby don't leave," he muffled out of his bleeding mouth. T.C. got a hit in, forcing me to the grown. The punch had my ears ringing, but anger wouldn't allow me to bow down. I picked up a wine bottle standing near the trash can. Smaaash! The bottle broke on his head causing a stream of blood gushing down his face. "Freeze, don't anyone move," I turned staring at the nose of the barrow of a gun that an off duty cop displaying his badge was holding. T.C. dazed, reached into his pocket, fumbled the silver mag, letting it hit the ground, extracting a bullet that went into a tree close by. The cop tackled and handcuffed him; then the officer phoned other cops for backup. We both were arrested.

WHO ARE YOU? SHEYLA……

M y anger was so severe that I had the Marcus Stunson kind of migraines. Getting that scene of Marcus and Tasha out of my head was impossible to do. Just hearing Marcus's voice on my voicemail disgusted me. I trusted him, and looked at him much differently than other guys. Tasha, well I shouldn't have put anything past her anyway, but it still hurt. He had the nerve to walk up to my job. No matter how he tried to get my attention, I just stared right through him. After Ja'Ron got away with that mess on me, I refused to go through it again. Even Tasha had the nerve to call me. It was like they were trying to throw it in my face. After ignoring one of Tasha's calls, I turned on the TV

> We have some breaking news. Terry Clemons and his lady assailant, Kim Patron were picked up and arrested in the local Detroit area. Terry Clemons is the fugitive police were looking for regarding connections to the death of Calvin Littleton. He may be linked to other local crimes in the area. An Eye witness said that

Marcus Stunson, star basketball player for the University of Detroit attacked Terry Clemons in what is believed to be in retaliation for his mother who was the young lady brutally murdered in the infamous Brewster Murder years ago. Officials from the University of Detroit wouldn't comment at this time. Tune in for the Six O'clock news update.

This is Rich Gatzer signing off for channel 7 news.

The phone rang right afterwards. "Ms. Patron or Sheyla," someone asked. "This is Sheyla," I replied. "I don't know if you're looking at TV, but the news reported information on your mother before we could get to you. Anyhow Kim Patron was arrested and is being held in the County Building downtown."

"Oh my God! Oh my God! My moms is safe!" Running out the house, I forgot my coat. Fondling with the key I stabbed at the ignition several times before the key fit. I was half excited, yet half nervous about our first encounter in years. My heart was pumping faster than the speed of bullets flying. I rushed to Grams church to pick her up from rehearsal. We met in the hallway leading to the sanctuary. "Grams come on," enthusiastically pulling her arm in the direction of the door. "She's here! She's safe!"

"Shey, are you alright. What's wrong with you?" Grams asked.

"My mother is locked up. She's down at the county. They found her!" We both rushed out the doors.

Waiting in the visiting room, I paced the floor. I held my moms in my heart, but the reality of seeing her now had my head spinning. The years of separated space caused me to question if this lady truly loved me. My palms started to

Retraced

sweat so I wiped my hands on my clothes. Then entered a woman with yellow stained eyes looking worn-out. I kept staring at how bad she looked. Her locks that once ran down her back was now cut shoulder length. Her forced smile revealed teeth that were covered by the residue of coffee and cigarettes; a complete shadow of her former, obviously shaken, her words were stuck. She stared at me, rubbing her hands softly against my tear-filled cheeks. "Ha' Hey, SSShey, how is my baby?" Her words meant nothing to me. She missed so many events in my life and had the nerve to ask how was I. I turned my head in the opposite direction giving the silent treatment. "So what are they sayin'? Are you going to be able to get out?" Grams asked to break up the tension.

"Well, they're asking me to testify against Terry, in which I could possibly get probation or a short lock up time. Hey momma Shey hates me huh?" Moms whispered.

"Give her time. It's a lot for her to deal with, that's all." Their side talk ended my silence. I stood directly in my moms face. "Time. We've already had enough time. I'm all grown up mother! You missed my entire high school experience. All because of a man. We don't have no mo' time."

"Shey you show some respect. She's still your mother."

"No momma. It's okay. I can deal with her," moms said trying to hug me. "Do you really think a hug can erase years of crying for your return. You don't even know me!" I said with tears falling off my face like Niagra Falls.

"Shut your mouth and listen to me!" Moms yelled. My eyes rolled up inside of my head. "I ain't gotta listen to you. You ain't my momma anyways!" Grams looked at me in disgust, "stop it! You betta stop it right now! Be happy you gotcho momma back and that the Lord kept her alive."

"Grams, is she alive? Cause it seems to me my mom has been dead fo' years." My moms eyes started surveying the room as if the walls would feed her more words to speak.

"Oh yeah Grams, Marcus is locked up to for getting into it with moms boyfriend."

"You mean that young guy who fought Terry," moms questioned with curious eyes.

"Mom that's my boyfriend, or should I say my former boyfriend."

"That boy really got wit' Terry. That was the first," moms responded. "What was that all about?" She asked. "That man you hid out wit' killed his mother. That's right Calvin wasn't Terry's first murder!" I yelled, venting my disappointment out to everyone around.

Not wanting to hear anything bad about Marcus, Grams got up from the table to go to the pay phone to inform Ms. Caroline of Marcus's arrest. Minutes later she came back. "No answer. Ms. C' is going to be upset about this one," Grams said.

"What can I do to make it up? I really love you," she said as Grams and I left, and headed down to the criminal booking station to see if there were more information we could find out about my mother's situation. That's where we saw Coach Thomas, Ms. Caroline and Marcus heading out the door. "Ms. C' where you think you going," Grams yelled out getting their attention. Marcus turned around showcasing his piercing eyes with the left one slightly swollen. "Shey I missed you," he pulled me aside to talk.

"I can't tell. Look like you had good company to me," I whispered, ready to let him have it.

"What are you talkin' about?" Marcus asked.

"You know exactly what I'm talkin' 'bout! You and Tasha," my voice escalating just a little louder than a whisper.

Marcus urging to separate even more from the crowd that included our loved ones said, "Me and Tasha. Wait a minute. Did you pop up to our dorm about a week ago?"

"Yeah! That's what I thought. You know exactly what I'm talkin'bout!"

Marcus braced up against the wall laughing uncontrollably. "What are you laughing at?" I asked.

"Girl, that was Dannie and Tasha. D and Tash are creepin'. Ha, ha, ha, haa, and you thought that was me, ha ha ha, haaa" Marcus cried in laughter. How foolish did I sound accusing my best friend and my man of cheating? Humiliation wasn't the word. I felt as low as low can get. "I'm sorry. Will you forgive me please?" Before saying a word, he grabbed me and gave me a big hug. "Of course I'll forgive you." We all walked out together instantaneously being confronted by the media harassing Marcus and Coach Thomas for answers.

What could be Next? MARCUS......

As soon as I was arrested, I knew the media was going to make a circus out of the whole situation. I was released on a misdemeanor, facing an anger management course and 15 hours of community service. Being locked up was a moment I'd like to forget. Me, Mr. preacher man locked up for not controlling himself. I knew people were going to judge me; I just had to be prepared for it.

A few weeks had passed with my name and reputation being slain in every media outlet. Coach didn't question me much about the situation until he saw it started getting to me.

"Son, I must admit I was very disappointed in you. You let your anger dictate your actions. The bible says we will get angry, but it tells us to sin not. You risked so much; your career, your life. Please think next time."

"Coach I know. But witnessing my mother's death, and knowing that monster did it, over powered me."

"One thing for sure, you need to get that insurance policy we discussed months back. If you were to get injured, that NBA money won't be there." coach opening up a juice box winked like he was teaching me something deep.

"Will they give it to me now?"

"Boy! What you've displayed on the court already got NBA scout's heads rolling. Barring any injury, you'll be a definite early pick. So don't get down on yourself, just learn from your mistake."

Hearing a coach give this kind of advice was unheard of. Most coaches scared of losing their star player tried to talk them into staying, but Coach Thomas really wanted what was best for me. Right after our meeting, I met with an insurance agent that handled athletic disability cases. He set something up with the NCAA, having me borrow enough money to pay the single premium for the policy that had a benefit of $1,500,000 for a career ending injury, and $1,000,000 in case of death, which was based on my projected worth in the upcoming draft. The only stipulation was when I made it to the league or collected on the policy, the money borrowed for my premium had to be paid back to the NCAA in the amount of $19,000. It was the newest phenomenon among top athletes.

That evening I finally got the approval from the university to do an interview with ESPN. They also let me know I was suspended for two games, which was against teams that were very beatable. "Well I just want to let everyone know that I made a mistake and acted out of character. My mother's killer was staring me in the face and I ignorantly jeopardized my life and others by not allowing the police to handle it." The interview lasted another 2 minutes, giving me the chance to answer the biggest question. 'Will the arrest hurt my draft status?' It was something I hadn't thought about, but I felt that under the circumstances, and the fact that I had a good reputation would hold up when character issues were addressed.

After the interview, officer Wilson from the 13th precinct called to tell me the gun they found on Terry was traced as the weapon used in the death of my mother. The only thing they needed was an eyewitness placing him at the seen of the crime. They were having difficulties finding witnesses for the other murder he committed. Apparently Shey's mom wasn't cooperating regarding the Calvin Littleton murder. It was a concept I couldn't grasp. Everyone was so scared of this guy, as if he was God or something. That bothered me.

DELUSIONAL DECEIT
SHEYLA......

Tasha was pretty upset with me about by accusations, but she forgave me. My life without her in it would've been so hard. We were closer than sisters. Tash sat me down and explained to me that she wanted what Marcus and I had, and she said Dannie presented that. Outside of Dannie's frontin', she said he was really a sweetheart. My girl was calming down, turning from her wild ways. God was really working in her life. She even started going to the church that Marcus and I attended. It encouraged me to continue to seek the Lord. Even still there was this big issue that continued to confront me; they call it lust.

There was always a need for me to have company present, someone to talk to. This day I was searching for complete solitude, so I decided to go to the mall unaccompanied. Plus Marcus was with the team playing at some school in Chicago. Broke as a joke, I found sanctity in window shopping. Working at the grocery store wasn't getting a sista what she needed. This store at Northland Mall called The House of Suave had some sharp clothes. Needless to say, everything was out of my price range. After

Retraced

trying on this out cold silk blouse, I pranced in front of the mirrors to see how fly I was. A voice in back of me spoke in a very decipherable, smooth-stimulating voice, "She'll take two of those on me." My eyes widened, identifying who was speaking. "When did you get out?"

"No hi Ja'Ron, I missed you Ja'Ron. Just straight rude wit it. Where are yo manners?"

"Anyways. Look, I like this blouse, but I'll wait to when I can afford it."

"Whatever. I gotta go, here's my cell number. By the way, you look real tense. I assume little Marcus ain't handling his manly duties" Ja'Ron threw 4 $100 bills at me while walking away with that stride that girls went crazy over. "I don't need his number," I thought, trying to convince myself there wasn't an immediate attraction. To regroup, I rushed to the nearest water fountain. Woooo, he was looking good. I swooped them bills off the ground, put them in my pocket and went home to add to my savings.

The cellular phone burned in my pants. One day I took it out of my pocket and stared at it. It took every bit of strength not to dial those seven numbers that could lead me into crazy drama. "Well I'm not doing anything but checkin up on him to see if he's okay," I thought. With Marcus on his road trips, my idle mind was making excuses to call Ja'Ron. I picked up the phone and slammed it down three times before dialing the numbers. Each number caused every sweat gland to react. The phone was very damp from my wet hands, so I hung up the phone again. Trying to divert my attention to something else, I turned on the TV. An image of a lady leading a man to her bedroom caught my attention. He kissed her on the neck as she lay across the bed. More perspiration exploded through my pours, resting on my forehead. As she removed her skirt, the flashback sent me retracing to a night I had with Ja'Ron, inundating my thoughts.

The phone became the focal point again. "Who am I

hurting by calling him," I thought. "Ja'Ron is this you?"

"Sheeey, the voice I couldn't wait to hear. I'm glad you called." I blew a sigh of relief.

"Don't think to much about the call. I just wanted to make sure you're all right. Plus I'm nosey. Now tell me how did you get out?" Even though I talked my self in believing the call was innocent, my body was nervously shaking as if I was sneaking to commit a crime.

"They didn't read me my rights for one, plus a few more technicalities induced by a little cash. You know the game. Nawhatamsayin'? Now let's forget the small talk and let me take you out for some grub," he said.

"No thanks. I ain't ready fo' all that."

This was the first of many calls within a two-week period. One time while on the phone with Ja'Ron, he began to reminisce about being with me. My emotions were overtaken by impious thoughts. I felt a strong desire to see him. In the middle of our conversation, Marcus came walking in. "Hey girl, who're you talking to," he questioned me with a smile.

"Oh, just Tasha. She is so silly."

"Tell her I said hi. I just stopped through since me and D' was in the area. He left, so can you take me to the crib Shey?"

"Tasha I'll have to call you later," I said playing it off, yet feeling guilty for talking to Ja'Ron.

The following weekend, Marcus had an out of conference game against Duke University. The team flew out Friday to Durham, North Carolina for the game. Duke was a well-respected school academically, but a powerhouse in basketball. They were the #1 team in the country. It was a chance for a national audience to see Marcus at his best. A game I was even hyped to see. The evening of the game I went shopping, but made a detour over to Ja'Ron's apartment for a quick visit, being it was on my way to my destination anyways.

"What brings you by," Ja'Ron opened the door revealing

his bear chest.

"I just wanted to see how you was living. That's all."

"And what if I had company?" He asked with a cocky attitude.

"I guess you just would've had company," I slid right by him and propped my rump on his couch without invitation.

"Well take off yo coat and get comfortable," he said scratching his head and smiling like he had me. He turned on the television to watch the big game. "What, you're a Marcus fan," I asked to spark a reaction. "Girl, please! I just wanna see Duke put that nigga in his place," Ja'Ron responded with much hate. ESPN was going through its pre-game presentation so Ja'Ron turned his stereo on to some slow songs.

"Shey come dance with me," he demanded. My song was on, plus dancing was my thing. I got up to show him how I get down. While hugging me, he began kissing me on my neck. Knowing my soul was being corrupted, I refused to fight him off, just giving in to his seductive attempt. One thing led to another, finding myself bottomless on the floor. "Jailbird, jailbird, jailbird was chanted by the crowd on the idiot box. It caught my attention in the middle of my betrayal of Marcus. Marcus was at the free throw line, and the camera showed a close-up of his face. I stared in his eyes and immediately came to my senses. What was I doing? "Ja'Ron get up!" He, being caught up into finishing, refused to obey my plea. "Ja'Ron GET UP! I CAN'T DO THIS TO HIM!"

"It's too late. What's done is done," as he forcefully continued, causing me to fight him off. "Look, I'm done anyways," he whispered while pulling up his pants.

I couldn't get my clothes on to leave fast enough. "Dumb move," I thought. Finding no serenity in the act I'd committed. The aching of my inner core fizzled out the two minute pleasuring of my flesh. "My Marcus. Oh my Marcus, I'm sorry," was the only thing my soul cried out for, his forgiveness. I knew my actions would have devastated him.

Retraced

The next morning the team arrived in Detroit after losing to Duke by three points. I met Marcus at his dorm room. "Hey, Shey," he spoke seeming emotionally drained most likely from the game. "How did you do?" I asked without looking him in his eyes. "I scored 36 points, but we lost. We lost and we had the game in our hands."

"Marcus can we talk in private?" Rationalizing rather I should tell him or not. There was no way for me to go through the agony of keeping a lie from him. Right when I was going to tell him, his eyes looking puzzled and gloomy wouldn't allow me to hit him with another storm. I just started crying uncontrollably. "Marcus, I can't tell you right now, I gotta go fix somethin'! Please forgive me!" I ran out the dormitory determined to clear my conscience.

Boom, boom boom, boom! The door opened. "I see you back for mo," Ja'Ron said arrogantly out of ignorance. "We need to talk right now!" Before letting him have a piece of my mind, the phone rang. "What up," he answered. "Shey this is bizness. Hold yo thought. I'll take this in my bedroom, when I get in there can you put the phone on the hook for me?" As soon as he entered his room, he closed the door behind him. "Got it," he yelled to let me know I could hang the phone up. Anytime he mentioned any type of business, I new it was something scurvy. Me being nosey, expecting to hear some girl on the other end, I pressed mute to listen in on the conversation. "Now what's up, dawg!"

"Yo I just came from hollering at T' and he need a favor from you."

"Go head, what's up," Ja'Ron replied.

"He's willing to drop you 60 grand to off somebody for him."

"Why me?"

"You did it befo', plus Ja, you owe old dude a favor. He got you outta jail didn't he? And he throwin' you crazy cash to get yo clout back."

"What's the name of the guy I gotta do?"

"The hooper. What's his name? Uuh, Marcus Stunson. You know my man you said yo girl told you was a witness and saw Terry kill his momma." I put my hands over my mouth controlling the scream I wanted to let out. My body wouldn't stop shaking as I continued to listen in on the entire conversation. "Ja'Ron you gotta get rid of him right away. Terry got all his witnesses to his other murders on locked. He found out the same dude he fought, attacked him because of that Brewster killing. This is the only piece of the puzzle left to get him off. Fix it right away!"

"I don't like the guy anyway, that's easy; just cause my mans tried to holla at my girl through the years like he wasn't wit it, and now they togetha. Tell T.C. I'll handle that now. I need to get that loot first, so I'll be by to get it. Shey told me Stun likes to jog outside around this time anyway."

"Yo' Ja', we'll give you half, then pay you the other half when you complete the job."

With my quivering hands, I lightly hung up the phone. Half crazy, half scared, mixed in with panic, not believing what unfolded. This whole time Ja'Ron was connected to T.C. I couldn't believe what I'd just heard. They were plotting to kill my man. Plus the conversation explained why Ja'Ron was leaving town all the time we were together, he must've been doing business with Terry the whole time.

In my panic state I quietly walked towards the entrance, Ja'Ron came out of his room. "Now where were we? Make it snappy, cause I gotta go make that money," he said as if everything was normal.

"Wwwhat money," I asked nervously looking in his eyes, searching for any sign of humanity.

"Shey you ain't changed. Look, I'll talk to you later, maybe we can do our thang again without you trippin', nowhatamsayin." He answered with a stare of demonism scaring me out of his apartment. I flew to my car going to warn Marcus on the hit on his life. My first stop was to the police station, informing them on what was about to go down. "Lady, Lady, calm down," one officer requested. "Look! Ja'Ron Black is going to kill my boyfriend."

"Maam, how do you know? Sit down and tell us what you know."

"You fools, we don't have that kind of time," I screamed while rushing out of the police department to warn Marcus.

Like clockwork, it was Sunday morning and Marcus always ran before going to church. My baby stretching and warming up, not knowing that his very life was in jeopardy. On such a sunny, bright morning, a cruel evil was right around the corner. I burned rubber driving into the parkway, "Marcus, Marcus, Please baby come with me!" I yelled. He asked what was I doing. "They're trying to kill you, come on!" I continued to yell at the top of lungs, straining every vocal chord I had. He wasn't budging, so I got out the car and confronted him. "Marcus, Terry Clemons is paying for Ja'Ron to kill you. You got to get outta here!"

"Shey calm down. I ain't worried about that guy. Plus look at all these people around here. He ain't that stupid. But that ain't the issue. The head cracker is how do you know about this whole thing?"

"Bey, this is not the time, just trust me!" I said, pulling him by his arm.

"Girl. What's going on? You came in cryin' this morning, now this. What's really up?" Marcus yanked his arm out of my hands.

"I was wit' Ja'Ron, okay! That's how I know."

"Wit'em. Wit 'em how?"

I started jumping and crying, screaming, nothing was breaking him. Every car that drove past frightened me to a shiver. "Marcus I slept with him. Now is that what you wanted to hear, I'm sorry. He's going to kill you! He's a murderer, please listen, please!!!!"

A blush of red covered his face, with tears running down his cheeks, "How Shey. How could you do that to me? I loved you! How baby? How?" Marcus took a step away from me as his words muffled together. I ran to hug him and he pushed me away, shaking his head in disbelief. This engine roaring like a lion sped up. "Oh my God, he's got a gun!" Some old lady walking her dog screamed. Like a scene from the movies, we turned, tink, tink, peoow, we heard bullets ricocheting off the cement and parked cars. My fear carried me to hide under my parked car. Marcus took off in the opposite direction to where a big tree stood. More shots scattered, causing zipping wind zooming passed my ears. The intense action was over in minutes. The car the bullets sprung from made a U turn. Thump, the car hit a man trying to maneuver out of its way. Ja'Ron's getaway driver lost control of the car, causing it to flip over. The driver was penned inside, while Ja'Ron got out and started running. The police wasn't too far behind, catching him not to far from the scene of the crime. The hysteria went to a simmer.

When everything settled, I turned to my left, noticing Marcus shaking and bleeding from his head. "Jesus no, Jesus no. This can't be happening." I cried running up to Marcus lying next to the tree. "Get an ambulance! Would somebody please help us?" Marcus body coming out of shock just laid there motionless, while I rubbed his forehead. "Baby you betta not be tryin' to leave me. You bet not." I used my blouse to wipe off the blood coming from his head. Finally the ambulance came and I escorted them to the hospital. The paramedics asked me to back up. After they worked on him for a minute, they looked at me and started laughing. "Uuuh, what's so funny?" I asked.

"Maam, come up here please."

"Boo! Did I scare you?" Marcus lifted his head laughing.

"Aren't you shot?"

One of the paramedic interrupted, "Ms., he ran into a

Retraced

tree. He was knocked out briefly. Other than a headache from the bump on his head, he doesn't have another scratch nowhere in sight." We laughed and I attacked him with a thousand kisses. The boy scared the blackness out of me. It was like winning a million dollars. After he went to the hospital for further test, the police suggested that we go to a nearby hotel under police protection just temporarily. They needed enough time to move Terry Clemons to a prison out of the state, detaining him without visitors until further investigation. Marcus told his grandmother what happened, but had to beg her to stay put. I did the same. "Grams, because of the incident, I'm staying with Marcus tonight, just to make sure he's alright." She was cool with it and was just happy that we were safe. On the news, they reported that Ja'Ron and his partner are facing 2 counts of attempted murder, 1 count of vehicular manslaughter, possession of a firearm, and more charges were pending. They'll never see the outside world again.

Lust + Time = Problems

"Marcus I know I messed up bad. I'm just so happy you are alive. I love you so much." I hugged him letting him know how sincere I was.

"Shey, do you know how long I waited to hear those words come out of your mouth. I love you too." Emotions overtook me. His naiveté had me captive in a sphere of repeated forgiveness. I grabbed his face with my hands forcing his face close to mine, and kissed his lips. His eyes holding back tears had me in complete attentiveness. Refusing to let his eyes focus on anything but my eyes, he started unbuttoning my blouse. "No Marcus," I uttered with little resistance. He laid me back, using his finger to trace my eyebrows. "Marcus I love you so much," came out of my mouth as a teardrop fell from his eyes, landing on my nose. His breathing got deeper as I concluded we were diving into a night of love. The evening progressed as the wind from the outside whistled a gentle sound of peace, putting the icing on a night that felt so perfect. Our night ended with us knowing each other like we've never known before.

The sun set, shining its rays on the side of my face, waking me up. I rolled over not feeling the body I laid with the previous night. I got up and peeked in the bathroom, noticing Marcus on his knees crying out to the Lord. Conviction set in with a vengeance. "Oh Lord! I am so sorry. Your man of God got caught in my lustful web. I didn't mean for this to happen. Jesus please forgive me." I bowed, knowing we had really messed up. Marcus entered the room looking sad. "Baby, I'm sorry," I said.

"Shey don't worry about it. We should've waited for marriage. It's my fought. I should have been stronger. Lord knows I should have been stronger."

The beauty of that night became very hazy, immersed in the developing relationship between God and us. We moved on understanding that we had to be wise in how we expressed our love. Avoiding tempting situations kept us on straight and narrow, really helping a sista like me to deal with the need of sexual intimacy. I felt so close to him. Marcus continued to love me, even with the knowledge of me betraying his heart. He made me feel like I was something great. Not once did he bring up Ja'Ron. It was me that held the shameful reproach of not cherishing what I had. Months had passed, and I became very ill. No matter how many times Marcus told me that he trusted and loved me more than ever, I continued to stress with self condemnation. I visited my mom at the county jail. What better way to pay Marcus back then by having a supporting witness ensure T.C.'s deserved punishment. I thought it would make me feel better. But after me and my moms last encounter, how was I going to get her to do me a favor?

"Hey mom," I said not knowing if I should smile or not. I felt like she would see the gesture as bogus, reading right through me.

"Hey Shey, glad you came back," she said.

"Let me be real and upfront. I love you, but you really hurt me. I'm not here for phony explanations. I'm just here for a favor. And if you want to start proving you're sorry for our past, you can start now." She bowed then scratched her head. "What must I do to show that momma loves you."

I folded my arms. "Tell the D.A. you'll testify against Terry."

"Baby, I don't know if I can do that," she said with tears fighting through her lashes.

"Momma please don't let T.C get to you. He's gone. We can have him gone forever. He almost had me and my boyfriend killed. For God sakes he the one that got you in all this mess! He ain't thought about you once in this whole ordeal. You gotta testify against him," I stood up heated, pleading for her to do Terry in. Her eyes ready to cry a river, "Okay, Okay, Okay, I'll cop a plea. But only if they can assure me he's gone for a long time." Her answer made me feel like a new relationship with her was worth a try. I mean deep in my heart I really wanted her in my life. I hugged her in relief as she rubbed my head whimpering, "Baby I'm coming home. Forgive yo' momma, please. Please baby." By bargaining, our hopes of her coming home real soon was in reach, and it would have brought some justice to Calvin and justice to Marcus's mom.

Leaving the jailhouse, I got in the car with the intent to tell Marcus and celebrate. The closer I got home, the sicker I became. I couldn't hold it off any longer. My plans were immediately altered, taking me straight to emergency. My body tired for no reason made me a little delirious. Mentally panicking I yelled, "Am I next to see the doctor!" The nurse pulled me in to get me from causing a riot. They ran test over and over again. Absolutely nothing, my vital signs were good. "Ms. Patron have you considered taking a pregnancy test," Doctor Quile asked. "Thank you Doc, it's time for me to leave. Thank you for your concern, but I'm straight." I stood up, threw my purse over my shoulder and strolled out like she had offended me. I was upset, but the more I thought about it, it became the only rational explanation. So I went to the store to purchase a home pregnancy test. As soon as I made it home, I ran to the bathroom without closing the front door. My purse fell to the floor as I ripped opened the home pregnancy test. I took a sample of my urine and placed it in the center of the test. Nothing appeared, so I placed the test on the counter and went to hang up my coat. The delay relaxed me, so I decided to check out the results. A blue plus sign emerged alone. I dropped the white little lying tester. I didn't want to believe the results were true. Yes, it was positive. The darn thing said I was pregnant. Scared straight, I picked up the test and drove like the world was ending. Marcus had to be in on the results.

Before he could open his door all the way, I rushed right passed him. "Come here and look at this!" I reached in my purse and gave him the test.

"Okay, now what am I suppose to do with this?"

"Boy! That is a pregnancy test." His eyes looked somnolent like he was going to faint. "It says I am pregnant. Do you know what that means?"

"Yes, yes, I do. I'm going to be a father," he smiled like he had won the lottery. It really relieved my nerves, because with his career and all, I thought he would be disappointed. He grabbed, hugged, and twirled me around. Like a flash of lightning it hit me. I also was with Ja'Ron around the same time. Embraced in this big hug from the man I love, realizing the baby may not be his hit me. I grabbed him tight and looked at him like it would be our last hug. How could I present this possibility to him? That night I went home emotionally spent. Grams reacted out of grace, holding me up in prayer. "Baby, just don't let this pregnancy stop you from making something out of yourself. What Satan meant for bad, God can turn it into good. We all make mistakes; trust me, I know."

Grams words were comforting, but the agony of not knowing who was the father was killing me. Everyday was more involved in worry; a yoke of self-inflicted bondage was tearing me apart. On top of Marcus being so enthused about the pregnancy made it even worse. When I came home after work and saw balloons and diapers on my bed, all sent by him, it ended my procrastination. He came over in Dannie's car with a dozen roses.

WAR WITHIN MARCUS......

I had just prayed for the Lord to help me in forgiving people. When someone said you might just get what you pray for was so relevant at this point. Shey broke some news that a brotha' wasn't quite prepared for. She cheated on me with a guy that hated me. It broke me like a horse. Being a man, I tried not to get emotional, but nothing could hold back my tears. My love was betrayed again by Shey. While trying to deal with the issue, we were interrupted by bullets. Ja'Ron was trying to kill me. Everything flashed before my eyes, Shey, my grandmother, basketball; I meant everything.

Trying to escape the whistling bullets, I ran into this tree. Not remembering much afterwards. The fact that I was breathing and talking demonstrated the grace the Lord had on my life. When I saw Shey's face in the ambulance in panic, devastated that I was hurt; my conscious dwelled on the love pirouetting at that minute, that second. All was forgiven. The passion that followed us to the hotel built to its peak of spiritual reckoning. Everything I believed to be right had no governing power in that heat of lust. We carried on the act of marriage, without the sanction of God. Yet I loved every minute of it. She was so soft and loving, but it ended with my spirit crying for God's forgiveness. I'm sorry, I'm sorry stained my heart. It felt like God wouldn't forgive me. I took a shower, scrubbing, using my towel like a brilo pad, as if it would wipe away my lustful actions. "Oh Lord, I'm so sorry," I cried out. Shey was a culprit, but I felt my strength should have carried us through. It didn't and failed both of us.

That Tuesday, I went early to bible class. No one was in sight, so I went upfront and collapsed to my knees. "Oh lord, forgive me. I was trying so hard to be an example, but I let me get in the way." My cry increased in tone, bringing Pastor Morwood out of his office to see what was going on.

"Marcus what's wrong?"

"Pastor I fornicated. I betrayed my promise."

"The Lord forgives the repented heart. It is now you that must forgive you. Don't you know we all fall short, yet he continues to give us grace? And Marcus, you have his grace on your life, now accept it and move on," Pastor said kneeling with a face of compassion. He and I talked all the way up until it was time for bible study to start. Right then I told the Lord that I was going to serve him from FROM NOW UNTIL . . .

Our talk freed me. I thanked the Lord for the benevolence of his Love. My goal was to show Shey how much God loves us. Feeling and knowing God's forgiveness strengthened my relationship with the one that held my life in his hands. Feeling Gods forgiveness made it easier for me to forgive. I was free, I really was. It was time for Shey to get free.

Shey was stressing on how she thought I looked and felt about her. No matter how many times I said everything was cool, her actions of over-pleasing was unlike the person I knew. I thought that stress was the reason for her getting sick. She confronted me with being pregnant and proved my belief to be wrong. "Pregnant," I thought. My seed, ready to walk this earth was a breathtaking thought. I knew the baby was conceived out of wedlock, but human life is always a blessing. I thought about the baby everyday, even on the basketball court.

One day playing in a game, at the free throw line it crossed my mine that the baby could possibly be Ja'Ron's. I shot two bricks from the free throw line. Right afterwards, I turned the ball over two times in a row. "Stun get your head into the game," coach screamed from across the arena. We barely won with me scoring my lowest total since the season begun. The possibility of the seed not being mine stabbed me like a knife. Withering off into a deep sleep, I had a dream of me as a kid without parents, running door-to-door trying to find my mom and dad. Before the dream was completed my eyes opened when the phone wrung for Dannie. "Okay Lord, I get it."

Shey called me over to discuss the parenting issue. Before she spoke a word I unveiled the dozen flowers I bought. "Marcus, baby. I've been thinking hard about this. There is a chance that this baby isn't yours. It kills me to think it's not, but that's the truth," she said looking nervous without looking me directly in my eyes.

"Listen. I thought about it too. Of course it hurts. I had a dream, remembering me being parentless. It helped me with our situation. The baby is innocent and will need a father in its life. I mean I want this baby to be mine more than anything, but either way I'll be here for you forever."

"Forever, do you mean forever ever, "she asked with a big smile on her face. Staring in her eyes I took a knee. "See this plastic ring is only a symbol of my love. When I get to the league, I'll replace this one with a diamond as big as Mt. Everest."

"Marcus what are you saying? Cause I'm not worthy of your love."

"Baby please, I'm asking for your hand. Will you marry me?"

"Yes, yes, yes! Oh my God yes, yes, yes! She screamed joyously. "Marcus honey, where are you from. You are not of this world, my darling angel. Spending the rest of my life with you is what I want," she continued tearing and just shaking her head in amazement.

LOVE FOR ME SHEYLA……

Marcus looked me in my eyes and proposed. His words brought a joy that I hadn't felt in years. How could a girl have deserved such a loving soul? That day was imprinted in my head forever. There continued to be restless nights concerning the father of my baby. I needed to know. Marcus assured me that he was in no rush, but I had to know. He said he had a dream that the baby was a boy and that it was his. He was so sure that it scared me. I mean was he tricking himself into believing such a thing, and if so, what would be the case if it wasn't. Everyday that agonizing scenario haunted me; the stronger my need to find out grew. I just wanted to get it over and done with.

    We later decided to elope. Marcus was a little worried about how the NBA scouts would view him morally. He said something about how they would do psychological test, background checks, and whatever to see how stable he would be living the NBA life. We came to the agreement that marriage presented stability, plus we were madly in love; and we just couldn't afford to hurt his draft status. Many experts were telling him he was a sure Top 5 lottery pick.

We knew people would advise us against marriage so we didn't let anyone know. However we did let Dannie and Tasha in on the secret to serve as our witnesses. Sunday afternoon came and we went down to Ohio and stood before the Judge. No music, no horses with carriages; just he and I holding hands, saying our vows. "I do," we both said in a hurry to kiss. "I now pronounce you husband and wife. You may kiss the bride," the Judge spoke us into a passionate celebration. I couldn't believe we were finally married. He promised me I would be his wife someday, and it happened. After getting married, I talked Marcus in getting a prenatal test to tell who was the baby's father. It took days of research to find out where the labs to do this procedure were. Only private labs handled this kind of testing and I had to pay out of my pocket. My insurance at the grocery store wouldn't handle it. The cost was $750 for the use of the laboratory and $2000 for a doctor to perform the procedure. Almost the equivalent of what I had saved to pay for my cosmetologist classes.

Before we could get back to tell our loved ones about the marriage; the media had already gotten wind of it. The news was broadcasted all over the local networks. Marcus was mad. Our grandparents were even more upset. Yet in still I wouldn't have changed a thing. It was well worth it.

Life Goes On

✤

Marcus had taken the team to the sweet 16 in the NCAA championships. It was a feat thought of being impossible. With more than 6 NBA teams needing a point guard, scouts were drooling over Marcus's stats; 26 points, 4 rebounds, 3 steals, and 10 assist a game. It was exciting preparing to become a NBA wife. We talked often about the kind of house we were going to buy. This was a frequently talked about topic, especially being I was still staying with Grams, and he in the dorms. June was the month of the draft. I wanted to have the prenatal test complete and out the way before Marcus contract negations were going to start.

The small office was set afar from the general public. As soon as Marcus and I walked in the double revolving doors I noticed a poster of a nurse hugging a patient with words on top that read, 'Our Love is in Our Care.' The bright, clean white walls reminded me of what I thought heaven would look like. "How may I serve you today, a thin bright eyed nurse greeted us with a big smile. "We're here for prenatal testing," I answered. There was only one patient in the building. Our wait was about a minute. They performed a biopsy to extract cells from my unborn baby. The Doctor set me up and took a plastic catheter, inserted it in my womb right through to my cervix. There was little pain. Marcus set still with a facial expression as if he was on a bumpy roller coaster. I didn't know if it was a result of watching the procedure, or the fact that we were in the process of finding out the truth. "Are you okay?" I asked. He just nodded yes. They took a DNA sample from Marcus and sent us home. "We will mail the results to the address you left us just like you requested," the doctor said, waving us out of the small office.

I'll never forget it. It was the week before the NBA draft when we received the letter. Both of our hands were sweating, nervous about the results. He asked me to wait before opening the letter. "Lets enjoy tonight and open the letter tomorrow." We went to dinner and just talked. He used his finger tips to massage his temple in a circular motion. Marcus frowned with every rub. "Baby what's wrong," I asked. "My head is pounding like never before. I need to get some migraine medicine." His headache worried the mess out of me. It was a sign that he was stressing over the results of the pregnancy test. What if the baby isn't his? Would he leave me? I didn't know, which scared the daylight out of me.

"Marcus are you sure you're okay?"

"I'll be alright, just a little nervous. I told you the Lord already showed me in a dream that it was a boy and it was my baby. So, I'm really okay, not worried at all," he uttered with a look of confusion. I knew his faith was slipping, even if he told me different. We went to the hotel so we could be together in privacy. That night we made love like no body's business. Everything was cool; this time he was my husband, so it was okay. Being pregnant limited us in how we could handle our business, but it still was a wonderful night. "Please believe me. It doesn't matter what the test says, my love for you is eternal," he whispered in my ear as I fell asleep in his arms.

Retraced

Morning came around and I woke up first. The night was warm so we had the windows slightly opened, causing me to wake up to a nice spring breeze. The breeze carried a smell mixed with air and seaweed lifted from the river nearby. I got out the bed and looked through the window. The sun glared, hitting me in my eyes, which caused me to shut the blinds. The birds outside whistled a sound of serenity. I stared at the envelope lying inside my purse; just hoping the results were favorable. I was so tempted to peak at the letter, but decided to wait until Marcus woke up. I sat on the edge of the bed just looking at my honey drooling massively, yet looking so peaceful. Refusing to wake him, I bought time by showering. The water splashing on my body didn't wash away the need to know the answer. After showering, I dried off, wrapped a towel around my waist and got in the bed with Marcus. I couldn't wait any longer. "Marcus, Marcus wake up please boo," I pushed him and he didn't respond. He was sleeping hard as usual. I rolled him over and was paralyzed by the sight of his eyes rolling back in his head. "Marcus, Marcus, wake up, wake up! Quit playin'!" His eyes focused on me then they would drift back up into his head. He was in and out of consciousness. "Oh my God SOMEBODY HELP ME!" I screamed opening up the hotel door. Someone in the next room ran out to see what was wrong. "Lady what's going on?"

"My husband won't wake up." We rushed to Marcus side. The man attempted to wake him, and nothing. "I'll call emergency!" The stranger looking concerned rushed over to the phone, mishandling it, trying to complete the task.

"Marcus we have everything to live for, you can't leave me! I need you, I need you, I need you!" When the ambulance finally arrived, they worked in a frantic state. "He has a faint pause," I heard the blond head paramedic say to the other. Reading their eyes, I had a lot to worry about. I rushed to throw on my jeans and a blouse, following them into the ambulance. I grabbed his hand, while his body jerked slightly. "What's going on? What is he doing?" I yelled hitting the paramedic in the back. "Ms. you must calm down. You're not helping the situation at all." I sat back just watching. Fondling my fingers like a schoolgirl, I couldn't think of anything to do but try to pray. My words wouldn't come out right. My thoughts were baffled.

Arriving at the hospital we ran through the halls. Entering the operating room, the paramedics and doctors stopped, "This is the farthest you can come. We promise to do our best." I clutched my chest, finding it hard to breathe. It took me a second, then I came to enough senses to call my Grams and she called Ms. Caroline.

They came in together screaming and crying. Needing more support, I called Tasha and Dannie. We were all in the waiting room hollering with tears of fear. After an hour of everyone praying and crying, the doctor came out. He didn't look me in my eyes, "Doc, what is it?" I turned to my Grams as if she could force the doctor to spit out what was happening. The waiting room went to a cease of movement and sound. "Mrs. Stunson, I'm Sorry, we lost him, caused by massive hemorrhaging to the brain." A force of rage raised my hands to push the doctor to the side and I rushed in the operating room. Marcus lifeless body was lying there. His arms and hands rested to his side. I kissed his lips. "Huuuuuh," gasped from his lips. It was his last breath. "How could you do this to me? Why did you leave me? Why?"

Like a zombie, I walked out to touch the facial skin of everyone in the waiting room crying. "Is this moment real?" I asked. This couldn't have been happening to me. I loved him so much. Tasha took me to the hotel room to retrieve our things, including the letter. I refused to open it until I made it home. I walked in the house with Marcus clothes hanging off my shoulder. His fragrance still fresh on his jacket caused me to go into another crying spell. Grams and Ms. Caroline were waiting for me. I dropped to my knees in front of them. They helped me to my feet. I couldn't say a word, just walked up to my room with each step being a hard chore. I turned on the TV. The news about Marcus's death was on every channel. It brought about more tears. My baby was gone. With all the years we had, I took advantage of most of those years. Love is a funny thing. It's not promised forever and it waits for no one. The thought forced me to retrace every moment we had. His silliness, the romance of him holding me, giving me tapes of love songs, the night we spent in Cancun, all of the special moments came rolling in at once. My body ached, my soul was drained; I didn't want to continue. I began second guessing if he knew I really loved him. "Did I show love like there was no tommorow? Maybe I took his love for granted?" I went downstairs crying again, "I loved him. I loved him so much."

"I know Shey. Here, I need to give you this so we can handle all the arrangements. Marcus had taken out a life insurance policy at the same time he got the disability insurance and had a will written up. The policy was for $1million. He left me $250,000 and you were the other beneficiary. The rest is yours," Ms. Caroline said with her voice trembling. Visibly shakened, she hugged me with massive tears running down her face. It was one thing I had almost forgot.

I ran back up those stairs and ripped opened the letter. There it was, 99.9% proof that Marcus Stunson was indeed the father of Marcus Jr.

Retraced!!!!!

Please visit for more on Retraced-
www.anthonycuffie.com

NOTE FROM THE AUTHOR:

Thank you for supporting this project. I've worked extremely hard to deliver this message of love. Most times we don't appreciate true love until it's gone. The purpose of this book was to confront love's enemy, lust and to fight against divorce. We're always looking for what will hurt us and not at what God has given us. Love is a choice, and I pray that you choose to love now, as if there is no tomorrow.

-TRUE LOVE BETWEEN A MAN AND WOMAN-
WAKE UP PEOPLE & STAY COMMITTED!
- Cuff -

If you liked the book, you'll love the soundtrack. The Retraced compact disc is full of memorable hits by Anthony Cuffie (Cuff) of 2ru Soulz Productions, Manifest Productions, and Noc-Noc Records!!